W9-ANK-500

"Everyone is looking for answers. In our world, many voices are offering solutions and it can become complicated to navigate through it in order to find truth. In *The 3 Essentials*, Casey gives a simple formula for activating the greatness inside you."   —Dr. Creflo A. Dollar

"In *The 3 Essentials*, Casey Treat highlights the three important ingredients we need in order to experience the God kind of success in life: Faith, Vision, and Renewal. By expounding on these biblical principles, Treat shows us how to overcome challenges, renew our minds and develop a brand-new outlook on life. As you meditate on these fundamentals, this amazing book will encourage and inspire you to live a life above mediocrity and settle for nothing less than God's best for you!"
                              —Kong Hee, senior pastor, City Harvest Church

"In his latest book, *The 3 Essentials*, Pastor Casey Treat skillfully weaves a garment of three important essentials—Faith, Vision, and Renewal—to help his readers overcome any level of mediocrity that may have infiltrated their lives. Treat provides insightful, practical, and biblical commonsense insights as a thread to strengthen the fabric of our relationship with God and others. With concise teaching, Pastor Treat gives us a biblical pattern marked by faithfulness and commitment, the spiritual keys necessary for every believer to become a positive force in his sphere of influence."
            —Marcus D. Lamb, president and founder, Daystar Television Network

"Pastor Casey Treat is a good friend, and an inspirational leader. His dynamic teaching style and desire to see people won for Christ and flourish in life reflects in those he leads and greatly impacted me as a younger pastor. I pray you would read this with expectation that God can and will speak to you about your destiny."
                          —Brian Houston, senior pastor, Hillsong Church

"Just as the human body has minimum daily requirements for vitamins and minerals to maintain good health—so does your spiritual life have basic, minimum requirements that are essential to success and effective living. Casey nails the three absolute essentials that will transform your life, shape your future, and make you a winner in every area of life."
                        —Rick Godwin, senior pastor, Summit Christian Center

Berkley Praise titles by Casey Treat

HOW TO BE YOUR BEST WHEN YOU FEEL YOUR WORST

THE 3 ESSENTIALS

THE 3 ■■■
Essentials

All You Need
for Success in Life

CASEY TREAT

Foreword by Dr. Creflo A. Dollar

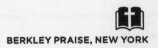

BERKLEY PRAISE, NEW YORK

THE BERKLEY PUBLISHING GROUP
Published by the Penguin Group
Penguin Group (USA) Inc.
375 Hudson Street, New York, New York 10014, USA
Penguin Group (Canada), 90 Eglinton Avenue East, Suite 700, Toronto, Ontario M4P 2Y3, Canada
(a division of Pearson Penguin Canada Inc.)
Penguin Books Ltd., 80 Strand, London WC2R 0RL, England
Penguin Group Ireland, 25 St. Stephen's Green, Dublin 2, Ireland (a division of Penguin Books Ltd.)
Penguin Group (Australia), 250 Camberwell Road, Camberwell, Victoria 3124, Australia
(a division of Pearson Australia Group Pty. Ltd.)
Penguin Books India Pvt. Ltd., 11 Community Centre, Panchsheel Park, New Delhi—110 017, India
Penguin Group (NZ), 67 Apollo Drive, Rosedale, Auckland 0632, New Zealand
(a division of Pearson New Zealand Ltd.)
Penguin Books (South Africa) (Pty.) Ltd., 24 Sturdee Avenue, Rosebank, Johannesburg 2196,
South Africa

Penguin Books Ltd., Registered Offices: 80 Strand, London WC2R 0RL, England

Unless otherwise noted, all Scripture references are taken from the New King James Version (NKJ) of the Bible. Copyright © 1982 by Thomas Nelson, Inc. Publishers. Scripture quotations denoted as "AMP" are taken from the Amplified Bible, copyright © 1954, 1958, 1962, 1965, 1987 by The Lockman Foundation. Used by permission.

Copyright © 2010 by Casey Treat.
Cover design by Judith Lagerman.
Interior text design by Tiffany Estreicher.

PRINTING HISTORY
Berkley Praise hardcover edition / September 2010
Berkley Praise trade paperback edition / September 2011

Berkley trade paperback ISBN: 978-0-425-24293-3

The Library of Congress has cataloged the Berkley Praise hardcover edition as follows:

Treat, Casey.
  The 3 essentials : all you need for success in life / Casey Treat.—1st ed.
    p. cm.
  ISBN 978-0-425-22571-4
  1. Success—Religious aspects—Christianity. I. Title. II. Title: Three essentials.
  BV4598.3.T72 2010
  248.4—dc22

                                                        2010017616

PRINTED IN THE UNITED STATES OF AMERICA

10 9 8 7 6 5 4 3 2 1

Jesus came into my life thirty-six years ago and I've been learning to live like Him ever since. He gave me four people who have helped me in this renewal process more than anyone else—my wife, Wendy, and our three children, Caleb, Tasha, and Micah. I dedicate this book to these four because, besides Jesus, they are the essentials in my life. I learn so much about the Lord and myself from them. I pray I never disappoint them, and may we all honor our Lord in life and in death.

CONTENTS

■ RENEWAL

FOREWORD

Dr. Creflo A. Dollar

I get excited when I think about the tools God has equipped us with to take our lives to the next level. We have a reason to shout when we know that we have the power to construct our lives and fulfill our highest potential! Everyone goes through periods in life when they wonder what the missing links are to reaching their destiny. Casey Treat is no stranger to that process of self-discovery. He is a man who has experienced the transforming power of God's Word and has allowed his change to impact others in a profound way. *The 3 Essentials* is evidence of his desire for people to unleash their potential and turn their dreams into reality.

Everyone is looking for answers, and in a world where so many voices are offering advice and solutions, it can become complicated at times to navigate through it all. In *The 3 Essentials*, Casey gives a simple formula for activating the greatness inside you—Faith, Vision, and Renewal. Through practical explanation, he clearly lays out how these three essential biblical truths are the foundation for creating success and fulfillment in your life. No matter your background, you hold the power to craft your future by implementing these principles.

I am a firm believer in the importance of providing practical solutions to life's issues. That is why I believe this book is such a powerful resource. Having a vision and submitting to God's methods of bringing it to pass are so important. The Word of God provides the answers we need. We must release our faith to receive them.

Now more than ever is the time to make the Word of God the reference point for everything you do in life. God has a specific plan for your life, and He knows exactly how to bring it to pass. By activating the three essentials, you will be in the perfect position to rise above average and achieve the abundant life He has designed for you to live.

—Dr. Creflo A. Dollar

INTRODUCTION
The 3 Essentials

As children we all dreamed of happy, successful lives. We saw ourselves as policemen, athletes, pilots, presidents, princesses, teachers, and more. We never thought of being sick, poor, addicted, or depressed. It was not until years later that we even knew of financial pressures, layoffs, bankruptcy, and sickness. No child dreams of a poverty-stricken, defeated life, but many people end up there. We get stuck in the battles of life and never find victory. Everyone wants to experience success in life, but many just do not know how. In marriage, in business, in family, in relationships, and in health, no person starts out on the journey with a desire to fail or to feel mediocrity at its best. Yet so many are struggling today, walking through life feeling unsatisfied and unfulfilled. Maybe as you hold this book in your hand, you are feeling this way, too. You know there is more inside you waiting to be discovered, that deep in your heart there resides greatness and the ability to carve a significant mark on this world. But maybe, too, you're not quite sure how to unleash those dreams into reality. I'm so glad you've picked up this book.

The truth is, as a Christian, you *do* have everything it takes on the inside of you to make every desire of your heart come true. You were created in the likeness and the image of God, and every aspect in your life can reflect the abundance and creativity of our amazing Lord. And no matter who you are, where you've come from, or what season of life you might be in right now, one thing is certain: God has more for your life and wants to bless you in a supernatural way. However, so often our human nature weighs us down and pulls us away from operating in the power of our spiritual nature. We begin to live our lives in the tempo and flow of the world around us, and instead of rising above every circumstance, we find ourselves pessimistic, focused only on our immediate realities, and stagnant in all realms of life.

These three attitudes are the exact opposite of what we need to experience God's best for our lives. Pessimism steals our faith in God's Word. Being focused solely on our current realities robs us of our ability to create a strong vision of our future and a hope that we will see God's blessings come to pass. As a result, stagnancy invades our lives and we fall into a deep rut of mediocrity and feelings of dissatisfaction. Life doesn't have to be this way! It's certainly not what God desires for each and every one of us.

I want to help you understand how to operate in and position your life for the God kind of success and prosperity. Let's turn our pessimism into faith; our short-term focus into vibrant, long-term vision; and our stagnancy into an acute ability to change and renew our lives. These are what I call "the 3": Faith, Vision, and Renewal.

After thirty years of pastoring over ten thousand people each week, as well as teaching all over the world, I am convinced now more than ever that success in life and our ability to change are based on three essential biblical truths. At every age and in every circumstance, these three factors hold the key to experiencing success. From the person who is just beginning their relationship with God to the Christian who has been walking strong for decades, these three are vital for continual spiritual growth. For the one who is struggling with addictions, the one healing from a broken marriage, or the one confused about their destiny, these three will guide them all to clarity and victory. And for the one building a prosperous business, the one seeking to enlarge their life with a fresh perspective, or the one pressing in to a deeper relationship with God, these three will springboard them forward to the next level in life.

Faith, Vision, and Renewal. They are not new ideas, but you will learn new ways to use them in the following chapters. Everything starts with faith; faith in God is the beginning of a relationship for eternity with Him. Faith causes us to see good things in the future and because of this we develop vision of success and prosperity in life. New vision causes us to realize that we must change and renewal begins to happen as we are motivated to move toward our vision. As you grow in your ability to appropriate Faith, Vision, and Renewal you will accomplish your goals and develop even greater dreams for life that you never dared to dream before.

No one thing can solve every issue in life. We have heard the sermons and seen the books of *the* secret, *the* answer, *the* key, and *the* miracle drug, but the fact is it takes more than one thing to deal with the problems and challenges we face every day. On the other hand, we don't want a list of twenty things that become so convoluted and confusing that we are lost in the system. Faith, Vision, and Renewal are all you need. I think you will see as you apply these three to your life that good things start to happen. Everything won't change in a moment; it took years to get where you are now. However, everything can change. With the right tools, we can see remarkable things happen. It is possible to overcome the problems, change the negatives, and develop a new life that is happy and fulfilling. To do this you need three things: Faith, Vision, and Renewal.

Without faith, it is impossible to please God, and this is simply because the only way any one of us can approach Him and begin a relationship with Him is through faith. We will receive nothing from God unless it is by faith in Him and in His Word. And until we are able to exchange all our doubts and fears for a life operated by faith, we will never get started on the road to a great life filled with true prosperity. As we study together about what faith is (and what faith is not), you will learn how to grow your faith to mountain-moving proportions. You will walk with faith and be able to utilize it as a powerful force to bring about the dreams God has placed in your heart.

The second essential for a successful life is vision. Proverbs 29:18 reads, "Where there is no vision, the people perish," and we can clearly see this truth manifested today all throughout the world. So many are stuck in their negative circumstances, boxed in by their limited thinking, and they believe there is no way out.

They have shrunk their visions down to a mentality of survival instead of one filled with hope and conquest. The reciprocal of this proverb is also true: Where there is clear and strong vision, the people prosper. When there is a vision of conquest, the people will conquer. Where there is a vision of adventure, the people will live daring and exciting lives. You can make your life be anything you want it to be, and it begins with vision. This book contains tremendous and effective tools to help you clearly define what your vision is today, as well as how to change it (if need be) to ensure you experience all God has to offer.

Finally, the third nonnegotiable essential for success is renewal. A person engaged in the process of renewal is one who has the desire and the ability to change. God is a God of renewal and is ever looking for new ways to bless and prosper our lives, but if we cannot learn to adapt to His plans, His twists and turns, and His ways of doing things, then we cannot receive His gifts. How many times have we said, "This is just the way I am" or "I've always done it this way" or "My family has always dealt with this issue"? We condemn ourselves to be the same and to have the inability to make the changes needed for the life we truly desire.

You *can* change *any* area of life you are dissatisfied with! You can have the successful marriage, the happy and fulfilled teenage kids (that's right, you read that correctly), the prosperous business, and the emotional and physical health you desire. It may take some renewal—and a bit of time—but the results are so worth it. The third section of this book is all about how to become new, how to think in a new way, and as a result, how to act in a new way. If you will apply these truths to your life,

I guarantee that you will begin to experience more joy and peace in your life than ever before.

In addition, at the end of each section I have included a manual to allow you the opportunity to immediately put these principles into practice. I want to offer you the practical steps to discover the fullness of life you desire.

Faith. Vision. Renewal.

If you will embrace these three vital truths, you will enjoy success, prosperity, and the overflowing, abundant life Jesus has for you to experience. "The 3" are not far off or impossible pipe dreams. We all can begin to walk in God's perfect will for our lives. "The 3" have worked in my life for over three decades, and I have seen them transform the lives of countless individuals in my church and people around the world. They will work for you, too. You can possess faith that moves mountains, a vision for success in life, and yes, even *you* can change!

Let's not settle for mediocrity. Let's not live in circumstances below God's expectation and design for our lives. Let's go for God's very best and learn to live a destiny filled with joy, adventure, deep satisfaction, and supernatural power. This book will show you how.

FAITH

FAITH

1 | Faith Is the Master Key

I wanted to speed. It was ten thirty at night, and the television broadcast started at eleven. There were hardly any other cars on the road, and I wanted nothing else but to put the pedal to the metal and get to Julius's apartment as fast as my little Volkswagen could carry me. The only thing stopping me was the scenario of a police officer pulling me over. Having a past record filled with multiple drug arrests and convictions, court-appointed drug rehabilitation, and parole, I was fairly certain I'd have a hard time explaining that my reason for speeding was to get to my mentor's house so I could watch a church television broadcast. True, I had lived the past three years completely clean, but my drug-addict-turned-Bible-school-student excuse probably wasn't going to fly, and the last thing I needed was a speeding ticket. So I obeyed the law.

Julius Young was the founder of Washington Drug Rehabilitation Program, and soon after I entered the program, he led me to Christ and became my spiritual father. For my wife, Wendy, and me, Julius was instrumental in many facets of our lives during this time, and I'll never forget the first time he introduced me to the message of faith. He called me late one Sunday night and said, "Big Red, you've got to come over here and see this guy on TV! He's a pastor from California, and he's talking about faith like I have never heard before." That was the first time Wendy and I watched Pastor Fred Price, and little did we know, it was also about to set a course for our future in ministry. Wendy and I did not have a TV, so every Sunday evening before 11 P.M., no matter where I was or what I was doing, I would drive as fast as I legally could to Julius's home so I would not miss one second of this incredible television broadcast.

Wendy and I were in our third year of Bible College. We were passionate about the things of God and studying to become ministers. Although we were spending every day in classes and lectures learning God's Word, we had never heard anyone teach on faith like Fred Price. He talked about Christians being able to use faith to take control of their lives not only to pray for God to do things but to actually initiate the change they wanted! He had a revelation that faith was not just a wish for God's promises to come to pass, but it was a tangible force to make dynamic things happen in our lives. He was strong and unwavering in his communication, presenting his teachings on faith as straightforward fact.

The message of faith came alive in our hearts. We ordered as many books and tape series by Fred Price as we could afford—which was just enough to get us started. We would pore over every resource that came in the mail, listening to and reading them again and again. The power of faith exploded into our lives, and the very next year we began Christian Faith Center, determined to spread this word of faith to as many people as possible.

Over thirty years later, I am convinced more than ever that faith is the master key for success in every area of life. It is *the* cornerstone and *the* foundation of the Christian experience, and without faith we are unable to receive anything from God. *By* faith we begin our relationship with God, *with* faith we walk every step of our lives, and *through* faith we can see God's promises in action. Faith gives us God's vision to see the impossible as possible, faith provides us strength to walk through the greatest storms of life, faith orders our lives and propels us forward in our destinies, and faith can change any area, from the smallest to the biggest, with which we are dissatisfied. Without faith, we will never see the full blessings of God. But with faith, we will experience wonders and miracles the world only wishes it could receive. Faith is the first of "the 3." To win in life, you must have faith.

Faith Is Not Religious

Think of the teacher who worked diligently to make sure every single one of her students succeeded. She was the teacher who around exam time would hand out the study sheet and say to the class, "Make sure you go over this sheet for the test." Then throughout the hour of review for the following day's exam, she would repeat that phrase over and over in multiple forms: "Study everything, *especially* the sheet I handed out." Or "Chapter 7 is important, but be sure to know everything on the *study sheet.*" By stressing the study sheet many times, she basically was letting her students know that if they came to the test with that piece of paper memorized, they would be sure to pass. She wasn't going to try to trick her students with clever multiple-choice questions or surprise them with obscure facts; she was telling her students exactly what they needed to know.

God is the same way. He's not trying to make our Christian walk tricky, and He's not about hiding secrets in the Bible so that only a few incredibly smart people find the "real truth." If this were the case, most of us would be in trouble. God is just like this teacher, wanting every person who comes to Him to succeed in every area of life. Throughout the scriptures, He made sure to spell out practical steps on how to succeed in every area of life: marriage, family, parenting, finances, personal integrity, and the list goes on. And when it comes to the subject of faith, He repeats over and over that we are to operate our lives entirely by faith.

There are four times in the Bible where God specifically repeats Himself in instructing us on faith ... four times! If God repeats Himself *four* times in the Bible, then He must be trying to tell us something.

- Habakkuk 2:4: "Behold the proud, [God's] soul is not upright in him; But the just shall live by his faith."

- Romans 1:17: "For in it the righteousness of God is revealed from faith to faith; as it is written, 'The just shall live by faith.'"

- Galatians 3:11: "But that no one is justified by the law in the sight of God is evident, for 'the just shall live by faith.'"

- Hebrews 10:38: "Now the just shall live by faith."

Like the teacher, God is making it clear: There are many things that are important, but if you make sure you know *this*, then you will find success. No matter what tests in life may come, if you have an understanding of *this*, then you will not fail.

As Christians, we must live every aspect of our lives by faith, with faith, and through faith. Faith is believing, trusting, having confidence in, and relying completely upon God. Faith is a lifestyle. In 2 Corinthians 5:7, Paul writes, "For we walk by faith, not by sight." The word *walk* here really means to live, to order our lives, to conduct ourselves by faith; not by sight or our natural abilities, our natural senses, and what we know in this physical realm. When it comes to faith, this is the biblical perspective.

To walk by faith means the decisions of our lives are controlled by our faith; our values and our morals are established by our faith. Our vision for the future and for our lives is established by our faith. Our financial commitments and the way we handle our marriage and kids are established by our faith. When we walk by faith we are not influenced by what's popular, by what's natural, by what's

> To walk by faith means the decisions of our lives are controlled by our faith; our values and our morals are established by our faith.

in the media or by what everybody else is doing. Everything we do, we do by faith in God.

Many people talk about faith: "Oh, she is a person of faith" or "Oh, yes, I have a deep faith." But when we take a look at their lives, they are living in the same debt, the same crisis, the same divorce and depression as everyone else in this world. They deal with the same addictions, habits, and negative attitudes that the rest of the world is dealing with. Many people say they have faith, but we never actually see it working in their lives; there is no evidence that would cause anyone else to say they are people of faith. If someone were to follow you around through your life recording everything you said and did, would there be any evidence that you were operating in faith and that the power of God was being demonstrated throughout your life?

Faith is not a passive belief in God. If the only evidence a person has to determine if we have faith is that we attend church once in a while, occasionally throw *God* in our vocabulary, and wear a WWJD (What Would Jesus Do?) bracelet, then that person would reasonably question our faith. In fact, many people go to church and carry around Christian paraphernalia but then have no other evidence of God truly working in their lives. Paul talks about this in 2 Timothy 3:5 when he mentions in the last days there will be people who will have "a form of godliness" but will possess none of the power that accompanies a life of faith. I call this form of godliness religion.

When I refer to religion, I'm talking about man-made things: buildings and icons, customs and traditions, that someone other than God invented. We have performed its practices or actions— good or bad—for a long time, but other than image, they really have nothing to do with God. Its repetitious prayers and motions may make us *feel* closer to God, but in actuality they do nothing to bring about a relationship with God. Religion says a church must look a certain way, a person must dress in a particular manner in order to be holy, and everyone must obey a strict set of laws to be in right standing with God. Religion is not faith, and it cannot release any of the power of God into a person's life.

God is not into religion; He doesn't care about buildings, clothes, or laws. He knows religion will never bring lasting change in people's lives and will never help them find the success they need. But most importantly, God is not into religion because it does not bring people closer to Him. God desires us to be connected with Him, to have an intimate relationship with Him, and religion will never be able to produce the closeness He wants. Only through the power of faith can we begin to experience a dynamic friendship with the Creator of the Universe.

Relationship with God Starts with Faith

A maxim I like to say is, "Sitting in church does not make you a Christian any more than sitting in a garage makes you a car." Many Christians confuse their religion with a relationship with God and think the level at which they immerse themselves in works and man-made law is the level of interaction they have with God. But learning about God, memorizing scripture, and even growing up in church does not create a relationship with God. Our connection with Him didn't start when we became religious, when we stopped smoking and drinking, or when we stopped any kind of sin. Our relationship, our connection with God starts with faith.

Ephesians 2:8–9 says, "For by grace you have been saved through faith, and that not of yourselves; it is the gift of God, not of works, lest anyone should boast." Paul teaches that we connect with God for eternal life by faith. It's not by going through Bible classes, paying the tithe, or any type of religious activity; our relationship with God is something that cannot be earned from Him—it can only be received from Him. By grace we have been saved, and it is through faith we receive grace.

So, God sends His Son because of His grace, and Jesus dies because of His grace. He pays the price, rises again, and becomes our Savior. That's all God extending His grace toward us. Then one day, you choose to believe in Him, to have faith in Him; and with that conviction, your relationship with God begins. Salvation came to you when Jesus died and rose again, but you did not receive it until you believed it. It took faith. Your name was on the gift of salvation like a present waiting for you under the Christmas tree, and when you realized that gift was for you—*blamo!*—the gift was yours for the taking. God didn't have to do anything the moment you believed; all the work was already finished; you simply received it when, by faith, you believed in it.

In Romans 10:8–10, we can find another description of the same process. "The word is near you, in your mouth and in your heart (that is, the word of faith which we preach): that if you confess with your mouth the Lord Jesus and believe in your heart that God has raised Him from the dead, you will be saved. For with the heart one believes unto righteousness, and with the mouth confession is made unto salvation." Our relationship starts when we have faith in God's grace. How do we know if we have faith? We believe in our hearts and we confess with our mouths that Jesus is Lord. We only need two things: a heart and a mouth.

Like so many other little babies, I was baptized, or "christened," when I was a few months old. I had no relationship with God; I had no faith, never believed in my heart, and never confessed with my mouth. I don't even remember the day. As a result, my baptism did nothing to connect me with God, as the following nineteen years would clearly prove. Getting my head sprinkled with water while wearing a white frilly outfit didn't bring me one iota closer to Jesus. It was not until I got an understanding of who Jesus is and what He did for me, believed it in my heart, and then confessed it with my mouth that my relationship with Him began. Religion didn't connect me with God; it was faith that connected me. *That's* the moment when my relationship with God began. Faith is believing and saying, believing and saying.

Throughout your entire Christian walk, in every circumstance, faith works the same way every time. Every blessing, every promise from God comes into your life by faith: believing in your heart and confessing with your mouth. When you believe in your heart that Jesus is your healer and you say it with your mouth that He took your sickness, carried your disease, and with His stripes you were healed (1 Peter 2:24), then His miraculous healing becomes a part of your life. When you believe in your heart God is Jehovah Jireh, the One Who Is More Than Enough, He meets all your needs according to His riches in glory (Philippians 4:19) and you say it with your mouth, then His financial help starts working in your life. Faith never changes. You can use your faith in many different areas, but it always works the same way. You only need to do two things: believe in your heart and say it with your mouth.

Everything God wants to do in your life requires faith to receive. He will never impose Himself upon you or force you to take anything He is offering. Consequently, every aspect of who He is, every promise He wants to bless you with, you must receive by faith. Romans 5:1–2 says, "Therefore, having been justified by faith, we have peace with God through our Lord Jesus Christ, through whom also *we have access by faith* into this grace in which we stand, and rejoice in hope of the glory of God" (emphasis added). Everything God has is accessed by faith! Access to joy, access to peace, access to strength, access to prosperity, to favor, to healing, to relationship, and to everything He has to offer! Access to God's throne room is available to me; all I need is my faith as the master key to open its door.

Faith in God is not some mysterious force, not just a good feeling that helps you endure life but does little else to help you change your circumstances. It's not something that just works after you die in order to get you to Heaven. Faith in God is a mighty force available to you to change your world and to affect the circumstances and the things you face every day: in the spiritual realm, in the soul realm, and in the physical realm. Let's spend some time learning about faith, reinforcing our faith, and growing our faith. As we gain understanding about how to use our faith, we will begin to see God's miraculous power flowing through our lives like never before.

2 | Faith Is the Muscle

"You have hepatitis C, and you are going to die in a few years if nothing changes." At the age of fifty, after over three decades of a strong Christian walk, and feeling like Wendy and I were just on the brink of exploding to a new level of ministry, this was the last thing I wanted to hear the doctor say. He continued to talk about what my options were, what my percentages for remission were (which were close to zero), and exactly what hep C is, but I don't remember much of what he said. But here's the interesting thing that I clearly remember: I wasn't feeling any fear—about *anything* he was saying.

I have to admit, I wasn't looking forward to telling Wendy about this, let alone the kids, but I wasn't afraid. The Treat family has always been one led by faith. Although at first there were a few tears, I knew we would face this battle with our faith. If you want the complete and detailed story of this season in my life, the year of chemotherapy, and how we all walked through it until finally getting a letter from the doctor saying I was completely cured, you can check out my book, *How to Be Your Best When You Feel Your Worst*. But I mention a little of this testimony here to encourage you: When you live your life by faith, with faith, and through faith, no matter what the world throws at you, you never have to feel fear.

For thirty years of my life, I had been speaking His Word and His supernatural healing over my body and my life. Countless times I had confessed Isaiah 53:5 and 1 Peter 2:24: "He was wounded for my transgressions, He was bruised for my iniquities; The chastisement for my peace was upon Him, And by His stripes I am healed." So, after receiving the prognosis, I didn't run home to flip through my Bible in order to find scriptures about healing or to see whether or not it was God's will to heal me. I didn't need to because by now I had them memorized and they were part of my heart.

I had been applying my faith for healing almost every day of my life, and that didn't change simply because the words were now *hepatitis C*. As far as I was concerned, headaches, backaches, injuries, pneumonia, hepatitis, these were all the same thing: issues that Jesus had already taken care of for me. All I needed to do was receive my healing by faith. But here's the deal: If I had waited to use or to grow my faith until the day the doctor told me I had a deadly disease, I probably wouldn't have been able to write a book testifying about my victory over it just a few years later—I'd probably still be dealing with the sickness.

Faith cannot be something you put on a shelf and then try to find in times of emergency. It's not a parachute that can suddenly save you once you've been thrown out of the airplane of life. If you haven't taken the time to learn about how that parachute works, how to use it, how to troubleshoot with it, even how to put it on properly, then you're probably not going to make it through the fall. And if you haven't performed some test jumps at lower altitudes and perfected the skill of freefalling and landing, you might have a pretty rough go at it.

> Faith cannot be something you put on a shelf and then try to find in times of emergency. It's not a parachute that can suddenly save you once you've been thrown out of the airplane of life.

In order to possess the level of faith that is ready for anything, we must use it every day of our lives. It's like the muscles in our bodies. They've been there since the day we were born. They grew as we grew, and how much we stretch and exercise them today is proportionate to exactly how much production we will get out of them. If we keep them active and strong, then we'll be able to do all kinds of fun and exciting things. But if we never move our muscles and we live a sedentary life, then they will become weak and eventually enter into a state of atrophy. Faith is the same way.

In 2 Thessalonians 1:3 Paul writes, "We are bound to thank God always for you, brethren, as it is fitting, because your faith grows exceedingly." I love this scripture because it teaches us that not only do we have the power to grow our faith, but we can grow it *exceedingly*. This kind of faith can overcome any situation that might arise, no matter how big or how small. Granted, it's a process that happens over time, but if we will exercise our faith muscles every day of our lives, then there will come a point when we stop and say, "Hey look at that—I have exceeding faith!" Regardless of where you are in your faith walk right now as you read this book, be encouraged: If you will just start to work out your faith muscles daily, you can grow your faith to any degree you desire.

This is a picture of what I'm talking about: Every day, you get up and say something like "Thank you, Father, for protecting me and my family as we go through our day. I'm trusting You will lead and guide me today and will bless and prosper my work. I don't know exactly what this day will hold, but I do know the Holder of this day! Thank You that I don't live by the world's economy, because I'm an ambassador of Heaven, and no matter what's going on in the world, I live above it. I'm serving You today and will be a light in this world today."

> Regardless of where you are in your faith walk right now as you read this book, be encouraged: If you will just start to work out your faith muscles daily, you can grow your faith to any degree you desire.

So then what happens when the boss comes and says, "Sorry, we have to lay you off"? Your immediate response is, "Praise God, I walk by faith, and I know You have an even better job waiting for me. This is my opportunity to rise up!" Or when the bank statement shows you are almost out of money? You say, "I tithe, and Your Word promises that You will open up the windows of Heaven and pour out a blessing that I cannot even contain!" Whatever the situation is, respond in faith, not fear.

This is exactly how Wendy and I have operated ever since the day we got saved. We started our church by faith, we grew in our marriage by faith, we had our babies at our home by faith, we believed God to increase our ministry by faith, we faced every challenge and every sickness by faith, we raised our kids by faith, we gave our finances in faith—everything we did, everything we do, is by faith! So when the doctor came and said to me, "You're going to die," we didn't freak out. We had spent decades of our lives building our faith muscles, stretching our faith muscles, and we were ready for the challenge. We certainly did not rejoice at the battle we were going to have to endure, but we were confident in our ability to walk through it. During the times when our confidence waned, we had plenty of people around us who would lift us up by their strong muscles of faith!

You can have the same kind of faith—exceeding faith. Make a decision to work out your faith muscles every day. Pick an area in which your faith is weak, and start there. Find scriptures that pertain to it, write them down, and begin to speak them over your life. Trust in God's Word and its power, and you will begin to see amazing results in your life. As you continue reading, I'll share many other practical truths about how to grow your faith. Use a highlighter, mark up the pages. Use this book as a resource for your growth in your walk with God.

Hearing and Hearing

The only way faith can grow is by hearing and embracing the Word of God. "So then, faith comes by hearing, and hearing by the word of God" (Romans 10:17). Many people have bought into the idea that faith is produced when a person goes through tests and trials. But this is not the case. Faith does not grow simply by going through problems or negative circumstances. In fact, I have seen many Christians go through tough situations, and instead of responding with faith, they get bitter and shake their fists at God. I have seen some people get completely wiped out because they had no idea how to walk through the issue by faith, and through the strength and power of God. Problems can definitely become an opportunity to operate in faith and to increase in faith, but this only happens if the person makes a decision to do so *and* if the person understands how to do so.

In the last chapter, I wrote that in order to live by faith, we need to believe in our heart and confess with our mouth that Jesus is Lord. Romans 10:17 explains *what* we need to believe and confess: the Word of God. As we study the Bible and go to church, we learn about God's promises and God's ways, and our faith begins to grow. Then, when we use His Word to guide us through the situations we face from day to day, we are exercising our faith muscles and becoming stronger and stronger in our faith. Notice I did not say we become stronger just by learning about God's Word. We also need to use that Word in our lives—believe it in our hearts and confess it out of our mouths—in order for us to see any results.

Romans 1:16–17 says, "For I am not ashamed of the gospel of Christ, for it is the power of God to salvation for everyone who believes, for the Jew first and also for the Greek. For in it the righteousness of God is revealed from faith to faith; as it is written, 'The just shall live by faith.'" The gospel of Christ is the power of

God, available for any person who will believe it—not the power for everyone, just the ones who will believe it.

Wendy and I have seen many people throughout the years who have come to church but have never locked in to faith in God. They sat through services but never really believed, went through the religious motions and nodded their heads but never trusted God. In-

> The gospel of Christ is the power of God, available for any person who will believe it—not the power for everyone, just the ones who will believe it.

stead, they were trusting in their insurance policies, the stock market, their doctors, and their bank accounts. They never decided to live by faith. Then as the years went by, we would see it show up in their kids, and in their health, and how they would respond when things went wrong in their lives. And every time this happens, we think, *Darn! If only they would have believed God and His Word, and had used all this time to grow their faith. They would have seen such a greater blessing on their lives, such a stronger ability to rise above the storms of life.* Again, the gospel is not the power of God for everybody; it's the power of God for the one who believes. Let's be the ones who believe. Let's operate in the power of God by believing what His Word says!

The passage in Romans 1:16–17 goes on to say that everything about our relationship with God is revealed from faith to faith; meaning, as our understanding *and* belief in His Word grow, our faith grows. Just like steps on a journey, each one moving us forward, so we move in our destinies from faith to faith to faith to faith to faith. First, we believe Jesus is our Savior, but let's not stop there. Why not believe He's our healer, our financer, our wisdom, our peace, and our joy? Faith to faith. Then let's believe for the spouse, and the children, and the raise, and the increase. Faith to faith to faith. Then let's believe for our kids' spouses, and their raises, and their increases. Faith to faith to faith to faith!

Every promise in the Bible is available to us; every aspect of God's character can flow through us, and along with these, an amazing power. God's Word releases a powerful message into our lives, and when we have faith in it, all Heaven breaks loose, all of God's blessings break loose, and we find ourselves living extraordinary supernatural lives!

Saying and Saying

And Jesus went into Jerusalem and into the temple. So when He had looked around at all things, as the hour was already late, He went out to Bethany with the twelve. Now the next day, when they had come out from Bethany, He was hungry. And seeing from afar a fig tree having leaves, He went to see if perhaps He would find something on it. When He came to it, He found nothing but leaves, for it was not the season for figs. In response Jesus said to it, "Let no one eat fruit from you ever again." And His disciples heard it. (Mark 11:11–14)

To move things along here, let me summarize the next several verses: Jesus made a whip, they went into the temple of Jerusalem, and He freaked everyone out. Then the next day, in verses 20–22, "Now in the morning, as they passed by, they saw the fig tree dried up from the roots. And Peter, remembering, said to Him, 'Rabbi, look! The fig tree which You cursed has withered away.' So Jesus answered and said to them, 'Have faith in God.'"

What? Peter tells Jesus the tree is withered and His response is, "Have faith in God"? I was stirred up by this response because it seemed like a non sequitur. What does the withering of the fig tree have to do with having faith in God? So I did a bit of study, and this is what I found: The Greek translation of this verse is literally "Have the God kind of faith." I love that! When a negative circumstance arises, the God kind of faith doesn't just sit down and accept it; it sees the challenge, speaks to the issues, and changes them. I believe Jesus was using this situation as an illustration about how we should approach life.

Anybody can talk *about* the problem. Most of us would've seen the fig tree and then complained all night about how hungry we were, and "if only that tree would've had some fruit on it, I wouldn't be dealing with these hunger pangs right now." We all act like this, don't we? We all have thoughts like "Oh, if only my spouse would be more sensitive," "If only my boss would see how valuable I am, I'd get that raise," and "If only my body would get healthy." Anybody can complain about what is wrong in his life.

Jesus wants us to understand that faith people don't waste their breath talking about their problems; faith people talk *to* their problems. We speak to those things that are wrong in our lives, and in doing so, we transform them.

problems. We speak to those things that are wrong in our lives, and in doing so, we transform them.

Jesus further explains in verses 23–24, "For assuredly, I say to you, whoever says to this mountain, 'Be removed and be cast into the sea,' and does not doubt in his heart, but believes that those things he says will be done, he will have whatever he says. Therefore I say to you, whatever things you ask when you pray, believe that you receive them, and you will have them."

Remember the example in the last chapter about the teacher at exam time who told her students exactly what they needed to know? Here is God once again spelling it out for us: "whoever *says*," "believes what he *says*," "has whatever he *says*," and "whatsoever things you *ask*." Four times Jesus tells us to open up our mouths and make some sounds of faith! Jesus didn't say we will have what we need, or we will have what we want, or we will have what we deserve. He said we would have what we say! Every day, what are we saying? Are we talking about things or are we talking to things? Are we whining about our problems, or are we using our faith to overcome them?

Have faith—the God kind of faith. How do you know when you have faith in God? You believe it in your heart and you say it with your mouth. If you believe "He bore my sickness, I believe I'm healed" (1 Peter 2:24), then say it with your mouth. If you believe "My God will supply all my needs according to His riches in glory by Christ Jesus" (Philippians 4:19), then say it out of your mouth. If you believe "My marriage is blessed, my career is prospering, I have sweet and undisturbed sleep and rest, and I have the peace of God that passes understanding, guards my heart, and guards my mind, so I don't have breakdowns and meltdowns," then say it out of your mouth because that is how we live our lives with the God kind of faith.

Let's grow our faith by hearing and hearing and saying and saying. Let's speak to our mountains and overcome every problem, every sickness, and every battle that comes our way. Let's believe God is our counsel, our strength, our wisdom, and the God who makes a way when there is no way. Let's walk strong through the cancer, the heartache, the loss, the financial downturns, and the emotional crises, and let's be examples of faith and power so the world will stand up and take notice. Let's live the kind of lives that bring people into the saving knowledge of Jesus Christ!

3 Faith Changes Things

Good thing the guy on the television couldn't see back at me because I was acting like a crazy person. When I hear Christians talking about how miserable their circumstances are and then blaming God for them, I just about lose my cool. And this time was no different. It was a Christian program, and the person being interviewed was saying things like "Why has God caused this to happen to me? Why hasn't He stepped in and saved me from all of this? Where is God when I need Him the most?" To all of this, I started yelling, "Use your faith! Where's your faith? You are not helping our cause here. Use— your—faith!"

This kind of thing gets me all fired up because there are so many Christians who love the Lord but are only experiencing a fraction of the kind of life God designed for them. Simply because they either have never learned to use their faith or they have chosen to not believe in the message of faith, they can't experience God's best. The real bummer is when they get themselves into bad situations and then blame God for not magically making all their problems disappear. These people just do not get it, and if you have friends like this—get each one a copy of this book.

So many Christian people choose not to spend the time to build a relationship with Jesus, and they live their lives on their own, by their own strength and their own wisdom. Only when they come to a place where there are no answers and they feel there is no way out do they turn to God. They say, "Hey, God, why'd You do that to me?" And this is God's reply: "Don't blame Me, I've been doing exactly what you have been expecting Me to do in your life: nothing! You have decided to be out there on your own, and you created this mess all by yourself. However, if you want Me to intervene, then all I'm waiting for is you! But here's a clue: Use your faith."

I've already written this in the first chapter, but I'm going to repeat it here—God cannot do anything in our lives except for those things we have the faith for Him to do. Every blessing, every promise, every aspect of God must be accessed by our faith. We cannot change the negative things in our lives simply because we don't like them or wish they were different. The only way we will be able to change and to overcome the problems, the bad habits, and the outside circumstances in our lives is for us to learn to grow and to use our faith. *Then* amazing things

> We cannot change the negative things in our lives simply because we don't like them or wish they were different.

can happen! Your faith can change *anything* that is negative in your life.

According to Your Faith

When Jesus departed from there, two blind men followed Him, crying out and saying, "Son of David, have mercy on us!" And when He had come into the house, the blind men came to Him. And Jesus said to them, "Do you believe that I am able to do this?" They said to Him, "Yes, Lord." Then He touched their eyes, saying, "According to your faith let it be to you." And their eyes were opened. (Matthew 9:27–30)

Faith will change the negatives in your life, but it is according to *your* faith. Jesus is the same, yesterday, today, and forever (Hebrews 13:8), and if He were here today, He'd say the same thing to us as He said to those blind men. If we said, "Jesus, can You help me get out of debt?" He'd reply, "Do you believe that I am able to do it?" Some of us would say, "Yes, Lord," just like those men. But some of us would say, "Well, in this economy, I'm not too sure. I've been figuring out the numbers for quite a while now, and I think, man, if you'd have just shown up a year ago, maybe so." To both groups Jesus would say, "According to your faith, let it be unto you."

Here's another example of what I'm talking about:

And behold, a woman of Canaan came from that region and cried out to Him, saying, "Have mercy on me, O Lord, Son of

David! My daughter is severely demon-possessed." But He answered her not a word. And His disciples came and urged Him, saying, "Send her away, for she cries out after us." But He answered and said, "I was not sent except to the lost sheep of the house of Israel." [Here, Jesus is referring to the fact that He was sent to minister to the Jews first and then to the Gentiles.] Then she came and worshiped Him, saying, "Lord, help me!" But He answered and said, "It is not good to take the children's bread and throw it to the little dogs." And she said, "Yes, Lord, yet even the little dogs eat the crumbs which fall from their masters' table." Then Jesus answered and said to her, "O woman, great is your faith! Let it be to you as you desire." And her daughter was healed from that very hour. (Matthew 15:22–28)

In other words, Jesus says to her, "Wow! According to your faith!" Do you have the kind of faith that even surprises Jesus? That's the God kind of faith I'm going for! This woman was bold, and even after basically being called a dog, she was not going to give up. When Jesus used the word *dogs*, He was talking about a theological comparison between Israel and the Gentiles and in essence was saying, "You are not really who I'm ministering to right now." But this mom was tenacious and came right back with "Don't give me your theology. I need help for my daughter, and I know you can get the job done." Her faith went beyond the adversity, the rejections, and

> Even when the world is mocking us and calling us foolish dogs, we need to persevere with our faith and never give up the pursuit.

the hurdles. Her faith overlooked all those setbacks and believed God would still work on her behalf. She aggressively believed Jesus was going to make it work, and His reply was, "Great is your faith! Let it be to you as you desire!"

When the doctor gives the bad report, when the banker starts to list off the interest rates and the debt ratios, and when your child seems like he will never turn around and live for Christ, we need to be like this woman. Our faith must overlook the obstacles existing in the natural realm and continue to see with eyes of faith. Even when the world is mocking us and calling us foolish dogs, we need to persevere with our faith and never give up the pursuit. Faith can change the negatives in our lives, but it is according to *our* faith.

Faith Can Even Sneak Up on Jesus

So Jesus went with him, and a great multitude followed Him and thronged Him. Now a certain woman had a flow of blood for twelve years, and had suffered many things from many physicians. She had spent all that she had and was no better, but rather grew worse. When she heard about Jesus, she came behind Him in the crowd and touched His garment. For she said, 'If only I may touch His clothes, I shall be made well.' Immediately the fountain of her blood was dried up, and she felt in her body that she was healed of the affliction.

And Jesus, immediately knowing in Himself that power had gone out of Him, turned around in the crowd and said, 'Who touched My clothes?' But His disciples said to Him, 'You see the multitude thronging You, and You say, Who touched Me?' And He looked around to see her who had done this thing. But the woman, fearing and trembling, knowing what had happened to her, came and fell down before Him and told Him the whole truth. And He said to her, Daughter, your faith has made you well. Go in peace, and be healed of your affliction. (Mark 5:24–34)

Her faith made her well! By her faith she believed what she heard about Jesus, her faith got her out of her house, her faith made her fight through the crowd, her faith reached out to receive her healing. I wonder how she did it. In that day, a woman having a condition like this would have been considered 'unclean,' and would have been forbidden to be out in public without wearing the proper identifying garments and keeping a fair distance from the people. If she had been caught, she could have been stoned to death, but her faith didn't care about the dangers. She probably got down on her hands and knees and crawled through the throng. Her faith caused her to do whatever she needed to do. She saw Jesus' hem, and she went for it.

I just love this part of the story: Jesus stopped and said, "Who touched me?" The woman had so much faith that she got what she came for, and Jesus didn't even know who she was yet! She snuck up on the Son of God and grabbed her healing, and Jesus wasn't aware of it until the moment He felt power going out of Him! That is amazing to me,

That is amazing to me, that we can have the kind of faith that can reach up and receive the blessing without even asking for permission first.

that we can have the kind of faith that can reach up and receive the blessing without even asking for permission first. She had heard about Jesus, and had gotten the revelation that if He would do it for them, then He would surely do it for her—even if she had to sneak up on Him to get it.

The disciples were confused; with hundreds upon hundreds of people pressing in on them all, how could Jesus ask, "Who touched Me?" *Everyone* was touching Him. But Jesus sensed something different. You see, a lot of people hang around Jesus, a lot of people are trying to get something from Jesus, but few people truly believe. Every single one in the multitude could have received whatever they wanted from Him, but they weren't using their faith to receive. That's why Jesus was able to perceive the smallest touch from the woman as her fingers grazed the fringe of His garment. That tiny gesture of faith made more of an impression upon Him than all of the other hundreds of people who were thronging Him.

Wow, let's be like this woman and have the kind of faith that stops Jesus in His tracks! Let's do whatever we need to do to receive from Jesus, even if it means taking big risks and crawling on our knees to navigate through a crowd. Let's use our faith so we can hear Jesus saying to us, "Son! Daughter! Your faith has made you well. Go in peace."

What Do You Want?

Then they came to Jericho. As Jesus and his disciples, together with a large crowd, were leaving the city, a blind man, Bartimaeus [that is, the Son of Timaeus], was sitting by the roadside begging. When he heard that it was Jesus of Nazareth, he began to shout, "Jesus, Son of David, have mercy on me!" Many rebuked him and told him to be quiet, but he shouted all the more, "Son of David, have mercy on me!" Jesus stopped and said, "Call him." So they called to the blind man, "Cheer up! On your feet! He's calling you." Throwing his cloak aside, he jumped to his feet and came to Jesus. "What do you want me to do for you?" Jesus asked him. The blind man said, "Rabbi, I want to see." "Go," said Jesus, "your faith has healed you." Immediately he received his sight and followed Jesus along the road. (Mark 10:46–52)

This is the story of Blind Bart. This guy inspires me for many reasons. First, he wasn't just sitting around like a victim someplace bemoaning the fact that he was blind. He was determined to do whatever he could with this life, and in that day and age, his option was begging. However, even in this, he was not content. He was always keeping his ears tuned to hear the chance for a better opportunity, and today was his day.

Just like the Gentile mother and the woman with the issue of blood, he does not allow religion, theology, or the acceptable social norms to stand in his way. He starts to yell for Jesus to come to him, but he is quickly told to be quiet by the people around him. As he heard the steps of Jesus getting farther away, he yelled all the more. Finally, Jesus stopped and asked for the man to be brought to Him. The same people who had just rebuked him were now rallying him with shouts of "Be of good cheer!" and they led him to Jesus.

Blind Bart was like a person on the *Price Is Right* game show who has just been told to "come on down!" He knew he was going to be the guy who won the new car *and* the Showcase Showdown because he immediately threw off his garment and came to Jesus. Back in that time if a person was ill, they had to wear a garment that identified their ailment. This allowed the Jews to know who was unclean and who was not, and who was therefore allowed to be among the people. Even before he met Jesus face to face, Bartimaeus knew he would not need that sick robe any longer. He was about to get his miracle.

When he got to Jesus, the Lord asked him, "What do you want Me to do for you?" I wonder if there were any snickers heard in the crowd. Wasn't it obvious what Bartimaeus wanted? But Jesus could not do what *He* wanted to do for the blind man, or what anyone else wanted, for that matter. It's only by *our* faith that God can move in our lives. Bart could have said, "Can you give me a new job?" or "I've been looking for a spouse—whom would you suggest?" And Jesus would have said, "According to your faith, let it be done unto you." But Bart got it right. He asked for his sight—and immediately he received it because that's what he believed by his faith that Jesus could do.

What do you want Jesus to do for you? Believe by faith and receive it. It's all according to your faith. What is your faith saying today? Is your faith saying, "I'm healed, I'm prospering, and I walk in the favor of God?" Then receive it. Is your faith saying, "My marriage is blessed, and my kids are growing up to love and serve the Lord?" Then receive it. If you agree with the world, and the prophets of gloom and doom, then please don't blame God when your life becomes gloomy and doomy. But if you will agree with God's Word, stretch your faith to receive the blessings found in His Word. Then you will experience the abundant life Jesus died for you to receive!

4 | Faith Takes Risks

When you hear the word *risk,* how do you respond? Does your face get flushed with excitement for a new adventure, or does your hand reach down to grab a brown paper bag in case you start to hyperventilate? If your life was to be made into a movie, would it be classified as an action thriller or a slow-paced slice-of-life film? So many of us were brought up to play it safe, to be careful, and to never rock the boat, but could you imagine what our Christianity would look like today if Jesus had lived His life like this?

My wife, Wendy, is a real risk taker. I've been blessed to have her as a partner in life and ministry because much of what God has called us to do has required both of us to step out with extreme faith. She's always been right by my side ready to take leaps off of huge cliffs with total faith in God. So I was surprised by what happened when I saw her reading the last pages of a novel she had recently purchased, and I asked, "Have you finished that book already?"

She smiled at me and said, "No, I'm reading the last few pages to see how it turns out so I can decide if I want to read it or not. If it has a good ending, then I know I'll like it, but if it's got a bad ending, I'm not even going to waste my time."

I just laughed and said, "You go for it, baby."

I can understand a person not wanting to give the space and time to a book they might not like. No big deal. But throughout over thirty years of teaching and ministering to people, I have come across countless individuals who live every aspect of their lives the way Wendy approached this novel. They want to have a guarantee of a happy, successful ending before they try anything new or go out of their comfort zone. The only problem is that a person cannot live a powerful Christian life if they have to *see* everything with their eyes before they choose to trust God. Everything about God and every aspect of our Christianity can only be experienced by faith.

In the New King James Version of the Bible, Hebrews 11:1 says, "Now faith is the substance of things hoped for, evidence of things not seen." But I especially love the Amplified Version (AMP) of this verse: "Now faith is the assurance (the confirmation, the title deed) of the things [we] hope for, being the proof of things [we] do not see and the conviction of their reality [faith perceiving as real fact what is not revealed to the senses]." Faith believes in something we cannot

> Faith is trusting even when we don't understand or when we are not sure what the end result will be.

see. Faith is trusting even when we don't understand or when we are not sure what the end result will be. Faith sees factual things which have not yet been revealed to our senses. Any kind of faith is risk, and if we choose to never take any risks, then we will probably never live by faith.

Now before you opt out, thinking, *Taking a risk scares me— I'm just not that kind of a person,* recognize that's not really true because you take risks every day. You wake up, get ready for work, and when you drive away in your car, you are taking a risk on the highway. You don't know for certain you won't get into a car accident before you make it to work or that the guy driving next to you hasn't been out partying all night. But you take the risk and go to work anyway. When it is lunchtime, you drive up to a window, throw money at a person who throws back a sack of food, and you eat it! Now *that's* a risk—you don't know where that meat came from or what was happening back at the grill while it was cooking. But you eat it anyway.

This morning, I took a vitamin, and I thought, *I don't have a clue what's in this thing.* So I read the box and still had no clue because I don't know what most of those ingredients are, let alone how to pronounce them. However, I take the risk every day, trusting that the people who made those vitamins are honest and know more than me, that they are actually filling the capsules with something other than sugar, and that by swallowing the tablets I'm going to feel better. So it's safe to say we are all risk takers in one way or another; some are just more intentional in their risk taking than others.

I realize it's important for people to feel a sense of security; it's part of our human makeup to gravitate toward those things that we think are safe, both physically and emotionally. Many times we put our trust and security in things like the government, Social Security, or our union affiliation. But, really, how secure are any of these organizations? And what kind of guarantees are there in the political, cultural, or economic systems in our various countries? All of these can rise and fall, can come and go, but there is only One who remains the same through any political turmoil, any cultural deterioration, or any economic downturn. Jesus and His Word are the sole foundations any person can put his trust in and build his life upon.

Water Walker or Boat Stayer?

Immediately Jesus made His disciples get into the boat and go before Him to the other side, while He sent the multitudes away. And when He had sent the multitudes away, He went up on the mountain by Himself to pray. Now when evening came, He was alone there. But the boat was now in the middle of the sea, tossed by the waves, for the wind was contrary. Now in the fourth watch of the night Jesus went to them, walking on the sea. And when the disciples saw Him walking on the sea, they were troubled, saying, "It is a ghost!" And they cried out for fear. But immediately Jesus spoke to them, saying, "Be of good cheer! It is I; do not be afraid." And Peter answered Him and said, "Lord, if it is You, command me to come to You on the water." So He said, "Come." And when Peter had come down out of the boat, he walked on the water to go to Jesus. But when he saw that the wind was boisterous, he was afraid; and beginning to sink

he cried out, saying, "Lord, save me!" And immediately Jesus
stretched out His hand and caught him, and said to him, "O you
of little faith, why did you doubt?" And when they got into the
boat, the wind ceased. (Matthew 14:22–32)

This is an incredible story, and many of us have probably seen
the painting of Peter walking on the water, beginning to sink,
and Jesus reaching out His hand to save him. But I think we
should repaint that picture to demonstrate what happened just
moments before, because more incredible than the image of
Jesus lending a hand to the sinking Peter is simply the visual of
that brave man who risked his life to step out in faith and walk
on the water! The rest of those turkeys stayed in the boat, where
they thought they'd be safer. I want to see a scene clearly depict-
ing these two types of people: water walkers and boat stayers.

Boat stayers don't need God to do much in their lives because
they are trusting in the natural supplies of the world, and they
don't think outside the realms of this context. It didn't occur to
the other disciples to get out of the boat; they were just trying to
wrap their minds around the fact Jesus was out there on the
water. Even after Peter jumped out of the boat and they saw him
walking, they still didn't think to participate. Any one of them
could have decided to join in on the miracle, but they didn't have
the faith. Boat stayers are analytical and try to figure everything
out *first* before taking any risks. They have to create a plan, a
budget, and other options in case the first one starts to go under.
They need to feel secure.

A friend of mine was telling me how excited he was about the
new health insurance policy his company was now providing. It

was an excellent plan and covered everything for his whole family. He was saying how much better he felt now that he had this and how much more security he had for his family. After he left I thought, *That's great to have a plan that covers all the medical expenses for any type of sickness. But what about all the diseases there is no medical treatment for? What about the conditions the doctors cannot treat? Where will his security be then?* I would rather place all my trust and security in God and His Word than in any kind of policy the world has to offer. I'm not advising we forgo participating in health insurance; I'm saying we should not place our sense of security in it. If we put our trust in the world, then at some point, we are going to be dissatisfied. When we have faith in God and find our security in Him, we will never be disappointed.

Water walkers, on the other hand, are ready and willing to jump out of the boat and take risks. Peter is the one we still talk about over two thousand years later, because he was the only one who was brave enough to step out with faith in the Lord's word. Yes, he did sink, but not all the way. The passage says he *began* to sink and "immediately" Jesus grabbed him. Who knows? Peter could have only sunk to his ankles or his knees—it doesn't say he gurgled out "Save me, Lord!" because the water was neck deep. He may have just barely started to sink before Jesus took his hand. Either way, the point is, Peter got out of his comfort zone, and the result was, he was able to walk on water alongside Jesus.

I'd much rather be floundering out on the sea right next to Jesus, attempting to accomplish something nobody else has ever done, than be huddled together with a bunch of onlooking boat stayers. I'd rather take a risk trusting in Jesus than play it safe back in that boat. Besides, who do you think was safer in that storm: the guy who had hold of Jesus' hand or the other eleven inside the boat being tossed around by the waves?

How many great companies have never been birthed because of a businessperson who couldn't take the risk? How many kids would have grown up to do amazing things except they were trained to play it safe and to choose the "sure things" in life? How many lives are being lived in a smaller way than God intended simply because these people were afraid to trust in the dreams He has placed in their hearts? What kind of person are you? A boat stayer or a water walker? The choice is yours!

Faith Takes Action

Everything Wendy and I, and the leadership teams at Casey Treat Ministries, have accomplished over the last thirty years has been completely by faith. Back in 1979, when we were making plans to start our church, we chose the date January 6, 1980, to be our very first service. We found a good location for us to hold services, a local Christian school in South Seattle, and we asked permission to use their facility. Before we had even been given the final approval from that school, we had passed out a thousand little yellow flyers advertising the date, place, and time of our first service. The next week when they called to tell us we could use their building, I thought, *Well, thank God, because we already passed out all those flyers!*

Maybe we acted a tiny bit prematurely, but we were on fire

for God and being fueled by faith. We weren't content to wait around for something good to happen for us. We were going to take action and walk by faith. Many Christians spend a great deal of time praying for a new start or a higher level in their lives but never actually step out and do anything to make it happen. They are waiting for God to do it for them, but as we have already talked about, God cannot do what He wants to in our lives . . . He can only do things for which we will have the faith for Him to do.

A few years after the church started, we sensed God telling us to start our television ministry. I walked into a Seattle TV studio to discuss the terms with the station manager, and I'll never forget our conversation. "Do you have a storyboard for your program?" he asked. I said, "No." "Do you have a script?" I said, "I have a Bible—that'll be my script." He looked at me with a smile and replied, "You have no idea what you're doing, do you?" To which I answered matter-of-factly, "Not a clue." I was just walking by faith.

He told me I needed to prepay ten thousand dollars in order for them to guarantee us any airtime. We said our good-byes and I'm sure he thought he'd never see me again. But he underestimated my faith. I left the station and went straight to the one rich man we had in our church and shared with him the vision of our television broadcast. He said he could give me a portion of it, and then I went to the rest of the church that Sunday and cast the vision to the congregation. The rest of the money was received, and we had the amount we needed to start the broadcast.

I walked back in the studio on Monday morning with

the check for ten thousand dollars. The station manager was shocked. "What's this?"

I just smiled and said, "When do I start?"

"You're *serious*?" he said, shaking his head.

"As a heart attack."

And the television ministry was launched. No equipment, no experience, no money. We had no idea what we were doing. We were willing to take risks, to take action, and we had faith in God.

I'm not saying any person should start their ministry or business exactly like we did; I'm simply saying that in every aspect of life—your career, your family life, your relationship with God—if you will walk by faith, God will show up and help you accomplish amazing things. He will walk beside you and do things you could never have asked or imagined, and you will be able to say, "God, you are so good!" But if you live the way the world suggests—play it safe, hold back, and never take any risks—you will never be out there on the water where Jesus is, and you will never feel God taking your hand and saying, "Come on, let's make this thing happen!"

Faith takes risks by taking action. If we are not acting on the Word of God in our lives, then our faith cannot work. Our faith is just vain words and empty wishes. James 2:14, 20 says, "What does it profit, my brethren, if someone says he has faith but does not have works? Can faith save him? . . . But do you want to know, O foolish man, that faith without works is dead?" In other words, faith without a corresponding action is void of any life or power and cannot bring about the promises, the blessings, and the miracles of God in our lives.

Every time God sees us serving and helping in our churches: ushering, door greeting, praying, helping out with the nursery or the children's church, He sees our actions and knows we love the house of God. Every time He sees us witness to our co-workers, love somebody in the name of Christ, feed the poor, or help the hurting people in our neighborhoods, He sees our action confirming our faith in His Word and His ways. Every time He sees us tithe and give a special offering, He sees we trust Him to be our provider. Every time we pray and lay hands on the sick, we believe He is our healer.

God responds to our faith and to our actions. Deuteronomy 16:15 says, "The Lord your God will bless you in all your produce and in all the work of your hands, so that you surely rejoice." It doesn't say the Lord will bless our faith, or our wishes, or even in those areas we know He wants to bless us. It says He will bless the work of our hands, in anything that we will *do*. The woman with the sick daughter was relentlessly persistent in her pursuit of Jesus. The woman with the issue of blood crawled her way through the crowd to touch the hem of Jesus' garment. The blind man refused to stay silent and cried out over and over to Jesus. Each person took a step of faith toward Jesus with a corresponding action. They received their miracle because their faith allowed them to take aggressive action.

What are you giving Jesus to work with? Are you just sitting and praying and hoping God will come and make a change in your life? Or are you going for it—jumping out of the boat—full of faith in the Word of God? If you do nothing, then He can bless nothing, but if you will step out in faith with some corresponding actions, then you will give God something to work with, and His blessings can begin to overflow in every area of your life!

5 | Faith Is for All Things

I wish I could promise that when you walk by faith in God, your life becomes easy and you will no longer have to face challenging or dangerous circumstances. I'd love for this to be the truth, but it's not. Even though we are Christians, we still live in a world that is under a curse, and as long as we are walking on this planet, we are going to have to deal with that curse. We are going to face weather crises like hurricanes, floods, tsunamis, and earthquakes. We will need to fight drought, starvation, and disease epidemics, and we will witness sin abounding in the world around us.

But here's the promise we as Christians *do* have. In John 16:33, Jesus tells us, "I have told you these things, so that in Me you may have [perfect] peace and confidence. In the world you have tribulation, trials, distress, and frustration; but be of good cheer [take courage]! For I have overcome the world. [I have deprived it of power to harm you and have conquered it for you]" (AMP). Because of these words from Christ, what I can promise is when we walk by faith and put our trust in God, no matter what situation we might face, we will have the ability to overcome it.

For those who are facing economic pressures, there is hope in God. For those who are walking through emotional scars and pain from the past, or who are dealing with sickness and disease, there is healing in God. For those who are facing failure in business or marriage or ministry, there is restoration to be found in God. For those dealing with addiction to drugs, alcohol, or pornography, there is deliverance in the name of Jesus. *Whatever* the trial or tribulation, if we will choose to operate in faith, to put our trust in God, we will be able to experience victory in our lives.

"Trust in the Lord with all your heart, and lean not on your own understanding; in all your ways acknowledge Him, and He shall direct your paths. Do not be wise in your own eyes; Fear the Lord and depart from evil. It will be health to your flesh, and strength to your bones" (Proverbs 3:5–8). This sounds so right and easy, but in actuality, it is very difficult to actually walk out. We like to "lean on our own understanding," in other words, have our own opinion, perspective, or way of thinking. When we face a situation, whether it is good or bad, we have thoughts and beliefs about it, and we act accordingly.

> *Whatever* the trial or tribulation, if we will choose to operate in faith, to put our trust in God, we will be able to experience victory in our lives.

We're funny creatures, too, because we want to believe we are right at all costs. If it is pointed out that what we believe is incorrect, even if the explanation makes perfect sense, we don't want to admit we are wrong. Somehow, that would translate into something is wrong with *us*. We have trouble accepting that we can be wrong and still be good people. If we live our lives caught in this trap, and face every circumstance and every decision by leaning on our own understanding, we will miss so much of what God has for us. "In all your ways, acknowledge Him, and He will direct your paths."

It takes more faith to admit we don't have the answer than to make something up. It requires more faith to say "I have no idea why this is happening, but I'm still going to trust in God anyway" than it does to fabricate some kind of pseudo-spiritual answer. When I graduated from Bible College, I had all my eschatology sorted out. I knew when the Rapture was coming and had figured out the millennium and all the various aspects of the last days. After thirty years of studying the Bible since then, I have come to the understanding that I know nothing. The more I learn, the more I know how little I actually know! Now, I don't even try to figure it all out. I just trust in God.

When Wendy and I were married in the late 1970s, we read a few books on relationships, took a few classes, and we thought we had this whole marriage thing figured out. We were confident we had everything we needed to make this thing work. While we have faced every challenge together and are stronger and more in love than ever, I still think I know less about how relationships work today than ever before. As our family grew and our kids matured, we kept facing new challenges.

Throughout it all, I learned, and I am *still* learning. It just never gets to the place where you know everything and you have it all "figured out." Every day, we simply put our trust in God. We don't lean on our own understanding, and in all our ways, we acknowledge Him, and He directs our paths.

We would be in trouble if we walked through our lives only by our own understanding. Every day we use inventions, gadgets, cars, and computers, and we have no idea how they work. Most of us have barely any knowledge of the technology we use throughout our day—but we don't let that stop us. We still enjoy these things in our workplaces, in our schools, and in our homes. Can you imagine how difficult our day-to-day experiences would be if we refused to use any product or invention that we did not have complete understanding of? We wouldn't even be able to get out of the door every morning! We wouldn't be able to use the microwave, the hair dryer, the car, or the cell phone. And our food—just like I said in the last chapter when I was talking about my vitamins—we have no understanding of how all our food is made and packaged or what the eighty-seven ingredients are in our energy drinks—but we consume them anyway.

So why is it when it comes to the things of God that we believe we have to figure everything out before we trust? If we are willing to *not* lean on our own understanding when it pertains to the products of the world, why do we insist we have to grasp every spiritual concept before we will embrace it and trust in it? I cannot tell you how many times someone has told me they were not going to tithe because they could not figure out how God was going to help them prosper because they dropped a check in the offering bucket. Yet they trust the mystery meat in the hamburger at their favorite fast-food joint.

Here's a better idea: Let's choose to trust in God at least as much as we trust in the world. Let's put our faith in His ways, even when we don't fully comprehend them. He's the God of the Universe who loves us, who gave His Son to die for us, who is ready to move Heaven and Earth for us, and is patiently waiting to spend all of eternity with us—I think we can trust Him. Let's not be wise in our own eyes, let's lean not on our own understanding, but in all our ways, let's acknowledge Him and then sit back and see what exciting things He can do in our lives.

But What If . . .

I was lying in bed one night, wide awake. I'm not going to lie about it; the reason I couldn't sleep was because I was worrying. I was thinking about our new building and all that needed to be done in order to complete it, about our finances, about how to finish the school building, and all sorts of scenarios these problems could cause. What if this happened? Or what if that happened? In the middle of it all, I felt the Holy Spirit bring a scripture to my mind: *Do not worry.*

My first thought was, *What? Who's worrying?* Then I realized, *Dang! I have been lying here worrying! How long have I been doing that?* Isn't it funny how you can be doing something and not even catch yourself until the Holy Spirit has to give you a little poke? I guess I thought I was just thinking about the issues, but the truth is that I was fully engaged in worrying. I took a break from my stress and began to think on the rest of the scripture the Holy Spirit was bringing to me:

> *Therefore I say to you, do not worry about your life, what you will eat or what you will drink; nor about your body, what you will put on. Is not life more than food and the body more than clothing?... Therefore do not worry, saying, "What shall we eat?" or "What shall we drink?" or "What shall we wear?" For after all these things the Gentiles seek. For your heavenly Father knows that you need all these things. But seek first the kingdom of God and His righteousness, and all these things shall be added to you. Therefore do not worry about tomorrow, for tomorrow will worry about its own things. Sufficient for the day is its own trouble. (Matthew 6:25, 31–34)*

As I meditated on these words of Jesus, I was reminded that worrying is a choice. The fact that Jesus told us three times in a matter of a few verses, "Do not worry," means it is possible for us not to worry. We can make a decision to do something different. That night, I made a shift in my thinking (aka worrying) and refocused my thoughts to God's Word: *Thank You, Father. You meet all my needs, and You take care of every part of this ministry. My steps are ordered by the Lord, and I am not going to worry about these things anymore. I trust in You and know You are making everything to work out perfectly.* And what do you know? The next thing I remember is my alarm going off in the morning.

I use myself as an example but think we all can relate. There are so many issues and potential problems every single day we can be concerned about, and it is very easy to find ourselves worrying instead of focusing our hearts to trust in God. Sometimes we will even buy into the lie that we cannot help it—"If I don't worry about this, who will?" But the truth is we *can* help it, and we can make a choice to meditate on the scriptures and the promises of God instead of our problems, our fears, and our doubts. When we choose to do this, then we will build our confidence in God, and our trust in Him will grow.

On the other hand, when we choose to spend our time worrying, we are building our confidence in the enemy. Worry focuses on what Satan is attempting to do in our lives and in the world, and when we are imagining all the bad things that can go wrong with our marriages, our kids, our money, our health, our work, then we are giving him power in our lives. We are building our confidence in Satan instead of in God, and very soon our worry will prove to us that Satan is more powerful in our lives than the Word of God.

Worry is faith in the devil. Meditating on the promises of God's Word is trust in God. Whatever is occupying our minds and our brain space—fears and doubts, or promises and faith—is determining who we are trusting: God or the enemy. Do not worry! Jesus said it, so we *can* do it. Do not worry, and instead, trust in God with all your heart.

You Have More Inside of You Than You Think

When my kids played sports, there were various seasons when I would have the opportunity to help coach their teams. I would tell the players that whatever intensity the other team brought, whether on defense or offense, they would have to match that level of intensity to position themselves to win the game. No matter what the situations were, they would need to face the other team with the same energy that team was bringing them. It wasn't long before I realized this strategy to win in sports is the same one we need to win in life. As Christians, if we want to see success in every circumstance of life, we are going to have to get up every day and match the intensity of the world with the same measure of faith, trust, and confidence in God.

According to 1 John 4:4, "Greater is He that is in us, than he that is in the world." This means what is inside us is not only able to match, but is also able to overcome, what is in the world. The good in us is greater than the bad in the world. The passion, the power, and the strength inside of us are greater than the negative demonic activity in the world. The health in us is stronger than the disease in the world. The prosperity in us overpowers the poverty in the world. The God in us is so much more *everything* than the devil that is in the world. Yes, in this world we might face some tribulation, but when we grab hold of this promise, we can realize we really *can* be of good cheer because Jesus lives inside us and can overcome anything in the world through us!

> The good in us is greater than the bad in the world. The passion, the power, and the strength inside of us are greater than the negative demonic activity in the world.

However, here's what happens to many Christians: They walk out into the world, and they don't match its intensity with the power of God within them. They listen to worldly songs, watch negative news, believe the bad reports, and very soon they find themselves twenty points down in the game of life with a back-ache and a headache, and they say they can't take it anymore. How did their faith become overwhelmed by the enemy? Because they started trusting in the world and didn't match the intensity of the world. Pretty soon, they become depressed, discouraged, and overwhelmed, and they think that he that is in the world is greater than He that is in them. Let's not let this happen to us—ever. Let's have this mind-set: The world can't depress me. The world can't push me down because when it tries, I push back!

When Jesus showed up, the demons would start to shake and quiver and ask, "Have you come to torment us?" The devil was stressed out because of the presence of Jesus, and He lives inside each one of us. Don't get stressed out by the world; the world gets stressed out by us. We don't get scared and intimidated by what the world throws at us; we intimidate it. We never need to worry or have fear because the life, the love, the energy, and the power of the Almighty God resides in us and is far greater than anything the world can muster up.

When the Storms Come

Some Christians believe if they have enough faith, they will never have a problem, but like I said at the beginning of this chapter, this isn't the case. As long as we live on this planet, there will be storms of life every one of us will face, and we will have to deal with those sufferings and those issues. But just because a storm strikes, that does not mean that we have to be struck down. There are ways to walk through storms with the mighty strength of God. We can do this in three ways, and I'm going to use some biblical stories of actual storms to illustrate each of the three.

Some storms we speak to.

When evening had come, He said to them, "Let us cross over to the other side." Now when they had left the multitude, they took Him along in the boat as He was. And other little boats were also with Him. And a great windstorm arose, and the waves beat into the boat, so that it was already filling. But He was in the stern, asleep on a pillow. And they awoke Him and said to Him, "Teacher, do You not care that we are perishing?" Then He arose and rebuked the wind, and said to the sea, "Peace, be still!" And the wind ceased and there was a great calm. But He said to them, "Why are you so fearful? How is it that you have no faith?" And they feared exceedingly, and said to one another, "Who can this be, that even the wind and the sea obey Him!" (Mark 4:35–41)

When Jesus was awakened from His nap, He simply spoke to the storm, and it calmed down. With some of the storms we face in life, we can just speak to them, and they will lie down. If an economic storm comes, and we speak to it in the name of Jesus, we will sail on by. If physical storms of sickness and disease rise up, and we speak to them, "In the name of Jesus, get off my kids, get off my family, get out of my house," they will quickly dissipate. Jesus said to speak to the mountain to be removed and cast into the sea, to not doubt it in our hearts, and what we say will come to pass. Some storms will be chased away merely by the sound of our voices, as the life residing in that sound chases off the death and destruction.

Some storms we walk through.

In the last chapter, we read about the account in Matthew 14 where Jesus was walking on the water while the disciples were trying to keep their boat afloat amid a storm. In the middle of the sea, the men in the boat were rowing fervently but going nowhere. This is when they noticed Jesus walking toward them through the storm. In this storm, Jesus didn't speak to it, didn't stop it, didn't change His mind about where He was going, and didn't tell it to do anything different. He just kept walking. Why did Jesus speak to one storm, making it cease, and in another, just walk through it?

I'd love to make up a really provocative answer because it would make this chapter much more profound, but it would probably be wrong anyway. The truth is I don't know why He spoke to one storm and walked through another. I guess sometimes we must walk through the storms of life by faith. When I was diagnosed with hepatitis C, I wish I could've simply spoken to the disease and not have had to walk through the eleven months of chemotherapy. It would have been awesome to immediately have that thing be healed, but it didn't happen that way. I had to walk through it—step by grueling step.

These are the times we cannot lean on our own understanding, and we must put all our trust in God. During these long storm walks, we cannot allow our minds to be consumed with the "whys" and the "what ifs." Rather, we must focus our minds on God's promises, match the intensity of the problem, and believe greater is He that is in us than he that is in the world. And when we are walking through the valley of the shadow of death (Psalm 23:4)—don't stop and set up camp! Let's keep our faith alive and keep on walking.

Some storms, we grab a board and hang on!

The last storm I want to talk about is in the book of Acts, chapter 27. Because this account is so lengthy, I'm going to summarize, but when you have a moment, read the story in its entirety, because it has the makings of an action movie. In this storm, the apostle Paul is on a ship (as a prisoner) on his way to Rome. At one point during the journey, Paul sensed they would face grave danger if they continued their voyage, and he warned the captain they would encounter terrible storms. But being a prisoner, Paul's opinion didn't matter much, so the ship left the port. Sure enough, they were met with a tempestuous headwind, and the ship was being rocked to the point where they were forced to throw their cargo overboard in order to lighten the ship and prevent it from sinking.

In Acts 27:18–44, an angel appeared to Paul and assured him that he need not worry, he would make it to Rome alive, and the Lord would save all the lives of the people on the ship. Now it seems to me, if God can send an angel to manifest and talk to Paul, and promise to save the men's lives, all because of Paul's prayers, then why couldn't He just have stopped the storm?

Again, I don't know. Maybe it was God's way of getting Paul to Malta where he started a revival that spread throughout the entire island. But maybe the Lord just wanted to have a nail-biter story at the end of the book of Acts. Who knows?

What I do know is that God sent an angel to prophesy to Paul and to instruct him about how to handle the storm. Throughout the terrible journey, Paul gives the crew advice on how to survive, and luckily, they all listen. Finally, the ship runs aground, and all the men have to swim to shore to save their lives, many needing to grab on to various boards from the broken vessel and float to safety. So some storms you speak to and they lie down, some storms you have to walk through, and some storms you just grab hold of a board and hang on for dear life until you make it to shore! Either way, whether speaking, walking, or holding on, when you put your faith in God, you will overcome in the end.

No matter what kind of storm you might be experiencing as you read this book, trust in God and know He is working it out on your behalf. He is leading and guiding you and is going to use this storm to perform something amazing that you may not be able to see right now. Whatever the circumstance, or the degree of its intensity, you can put your faith and your entire life in the hands of your Heavenly Father. He loves you and wants to bring success in your life even more than you do! If you decide to place your trust in the things of this world, you will surely be disappointed, but if you will choose to lean not on your own understanding, and in all your ways acknowledge Him, then He will direct every step of your path, and very soon you will experience wonderful success.

Faith is the first of "the 3." It is the premiere ingredient in our

Christian lives and *nothing* of eternal value can be accomplished without it. It grows in our hearts as we listen and study the Word, it is activated in our lives through our confession, and faith is seen in our lives by the supernatural fruit it produces. *You* are a person of faith. Never underestimate the power of faith residing inside of you. Remember, it's not a feeling; it's an attitude and unwavering belief in God.

My desire is not just to offer you teaching about what faith is, but also to give you a practical resource to mature and strengthen your personal faith. The Faith Manual, which follows, is a valuable resource designed to help you do just that. It is full of confessions for you to speak over your life and your circumstances. Starting with a few longer, general faith confessions for your life, as you continue through the manual, you'll find confessions listed in topical form. Faith people don't speak *about* their problems; faith people speak *to* their problems! As you utilize this resource I know you will see incredible transformation begin to take place in those areas you never thought possible.

FAITH MANUAL

FAITH MANUAL

Faith Confessions

God's Word

The Bible is the Word of God and I believe it. I am what it says I am, I have what it says I have, and I can do what it says I can do. I am being transformed by the renewing of my mind. Today I will take another step toward God's perfect will. I'm becoming like Jesus; I'm energized by the Holy Spirit; I have the desire, discipline, and determination to be all God has called me to be.

Ministry

The Spirit of the Lord is upon me because He has anointed me to preach the gospel to the poor. He has sent me to heal the brokenhearted, to preach deliverance to the captives, and the recovering of sight to the blind, to set at liberty those who are bruised, and to preach the acceptable year of the Lord. Jesus is made unto me wisdom, righteousness, sanctification, and redemption. If I lack wisdom, I ask of God who gives to all men liberally and without reproach, and it is given to me. I walk in love. The love of God is shed abroad in my heart by the Holy Spirit. I have been made the righteousness of God in Christ. Whatever I do shall prosper, for I prosper and live in health, even as my soul prospers. I tread on serpents and scorpions and over all the power of the enemy. Nothing shall by any means hurt me, for the joy of the Lord is my strength.

(Nehemiah 8:10; Luke 4:18; Luke 10:19; Romans 5:5; 1 Corinthians 1:30; 2 Corinthians 5:21; James 1:5; 3 John 2)

Personal Commitment and Discipline

I am a disciplined man/woman of God. I give myself continually to prayer and to the ministry of God, a workman who need not be ashamed, rightly dividing the Word of truth. I am not conformed to this world, but transformed by the renewing of my mind, to prove what is that good, acceptable, and perfect will of God. I am risen with Christ. I set my mind on things above, not on the things on this earth. I seek those things which are above where Christ sits on the right hand of God. Whatsoever things are true, honest, just, pure, lovely, of good report, virtuous, and praiseworthy, these are the only things on which I fix my mind.

I love [spouse's name] as Jesus loved the church and gave Himself for it. We walk in harmony and in one accord. We have been made one by the Spirit of God. I love [children's names]. I train them in the way they should go, and when they are old they will not depart from it. I raise them up in the nurture and the admonition of the Lord.

My body is the temple of the Holy Spirit. No evil shall befall me, neither shall any plague come near my dwelling. By the stripes of Jesus I am healed. I am blessed with the blessings of Abraham. I am very rich in silver and in gold. The blessing of the Lord makes me rich and He adds no sorrow to it. I prosper and live in health even as my soul prospers. As He who has called me is holy, so I am holy in all manner of lifestyle because it is written, "Be holy for I am holy."

I put aside my old ways of thinking and acting, which are corrupt according to the deceitful lusts. I am renewed in the spirit of my mind and put on the new man, which after God is created in righteousness and true holiness. I am strong and very courageous. The Word of God shall not depart out of my mouth, but I meditate therein day and night to observe to do according to all that is written therein. Then I make my way prosperous and then I have good success.

(Genesis 49:26 [AMP]; Joshua 1:7–8; Psalm 91:10; Proverbs 10:22; Proverbs 22:6; Acts 6:4; Romans 12:2; 1 Corinthians 3:16; Ephesians 4:22–24; Ephesians 5:25; Ephesians 6:4; Philippians 4:8; Colossians 3:1–2; 2 Timothy 2:15; 1 Peter 1:15–16; 1 Peter 2:24)

Wisdom, Knowledge, and the Direction of God

I do not seek after riches, wealth, or honor, but I seek for wisdom and knowledge that are granted unto me, and I believe You have given riches, wealth, and honor according to Your Word. Wisdom is the principal thing, therefore I get wisdom, and with all my getting I get understanding. I exalt Wisdom and she promotes me. She'll bring me to honor when I embrace her.

Happy is the man who finds wisdom and the man who gets understanding, for the merchandise of it is better than the merchandise of silver, and the gain thereof better than fine gold. Wisdom is more precious than rubies and all the things I can desire are not to be compared to her. Length of days is in her right hand and in her left hand are riches and honor. She is the tree of life to them that lay hold upon her. Happy is everyone who retains her. The Lord by wisdom has founded the earth, by understanding has He established the heavens. I am willing and obedient, and I eat the best the land has to offer. I seek first the kingdom of God and His righteousness, and all these other things are added unto me. I am a blessed man/woman who walks not in the counsel of the ungodly, nor stands in the way of sinners, nor sits in the seat of the scornful. But my delight is in the law of the Lord, and in Your law do I meditate day and night. I am like a tree planted by rivers of water that brings forth fruit in season. My leaf also shall not wither and whatever I do shall prosper.

(2 Chronicles 1:12; Psalm 1:1–3; Proverbs 3:13–19; Proverbs 4:7–8; Isaiah 1:19; Matthew 6:33)

Topical Faith Confessions

Overcoming Anger

I am a person who is not given to anger, and I put away all wrath, anger, clamor, bitterness, and evil speaking. When I feel anger rising, I do not yield to it nor do I sin in it. I know that a soft answer turns away wrath, and I focus on being a kind, tender-hearted, and forgiving person to all those around me.
(Ephesians 4:26, 31–32; Proverbs 15:1)

Developing Boldness

The righteous are as bold as a lion, and that means me! I do not shirk away from challenges or situations because I am filled with the strength of God. I can do all things through Christ who infuses me on the inside with mighty power. I choose this day to be a person who can look others in the eye and who can speak up when needed. I walk by faith and not by what I see or how I feel.

(Proverbs 28:1; Philippians 4:13; Romans 1:17)

Succeeding in Business

I am a child of God, and I am blessed with the blessing of Abraham. God will set me up on high, give me His favor, and His blessings shall overtake me. Blessed will I be going in, and blessed will I be going out. Everything I set my hands to will prosper. I operate my affairs with the wisdom of God every day because I know when I do, I will make my way prosperous.

(Deuteronomy 28:1–3, 5, 8; Joshua 1:8)

Finding Comfort

I do not allow my heart to be troubled because I trust in Jesus. The Lord is my shepherd, and He takes care of my every need. When I am anxious, He leads me beside still waters; when I am weak, He restores my soul. Even during the times it feels like I'm walking through the valley of the shadow of death, I trust He is right beside me, leading and guiding me through to victory. In the world, I will sometimes have tribulation, but I can be of good

cheer because Jesus has overcome the world, and He lives inside of me.
(Psalm 23; John 14:1, 16:33)

Dealing with Condemnation

I am in Christ Jesus, so I do not need to allow condemnation to be a part of my life. I will not let guilt or thoughts of past failures rule my heart and mind. I am righteous in Christ, and I walk in the spirit of freedom and not the flesh of condemnation.
(Romans 8:1–2)

Building Courage

I am strong and very courageous, for God Almighty is with me wherever I go. He will never leave me or forsake me; therefore I never need to fear any person or any situation. And even in the midst of feeling fear, the courageous stand strong and walk forward into destiny anyway!
(Joshua 1:7–9)

Discovering Destiny

When I delight myself in the Lord, He gives me the desires of my heart. I trust that my every step is ordered by the Lord. I am

God's workmanship, created in Christ Jesus, for good works which God predestined just for me. He has a plan and purpose for my life, and His thoughts for me are for good and not evil so that I can have hope for my entire life.

(Psalm 37:4; Proverbs 20:24; Ephesians 2:10; Jeremiah 29:11)

Fighting Fear

God has not given me a spirit of fear or cowardice or timidity; He has given me a spirit of power, love, and a sound and well-balanced mind. The God of the Universe is my Light and my Salvation, my Refuge and the Stronghold of my life—what can possibly harm me? Because God is with me, I do not fear when sudden terror rises in my heart; I realize it is just a feeling. I'm not afraid of sickness or disease, or that sudden death will touch me. A thousand may fall at my side, and ten thousand at my right hand, but it will not come near me because I dwell in the secret place of the Most High God.

(2 Timothy 1:7; Psalm 27:1; Psalm 91:1, 5–7)

Receiving Finances

God gives me power to get wealth so that through me He can establish His covenant throughout the earth. I do not operate according to the financial systems of the world so I do not need to worry about anything. I operate according to God's financial system; I honor Him with my tithe and my offerings, and He supplies my needs according to His riches in glory by Christ Jesus.

(Deuteronomy 8:18; Proverbs 3:9; Philippians 4:19)

Experiencing Healing

Jesus was sent by the Father to undo all that Satan had done, and this includes overcoming sickness and disease. He was wounded for my sins and bruised for my iniquities, and by His stripes, we were healed. This includes any kind of physical, emotional, or mental pain or disease. As my soul prospers in Christ, my body also prospers and is free from sickness. Jesus went about healing all who were sick when He walked on the earth, and He is the same yesterday, today, and forever, so I can expect His healing to be at work in my life right now.

(Isaiah 53:5; 2 Peter 2:24; 3 John 2, Hebrews 13:8)

Walking in Joy

Today I choose to walk in the joy of the Lord, because His joy is my strength. I will count it joy, even when I face tests and trials because they are only temporary and will produce patience and endurance in my life. In God's presence is fullness of joy, and at His right hand are pleasures forevermore.

(Nehemiah 8:10; James 1:2; Psalm 16:11)

Cultivating Love

Love is an action, not a feeling, and I am a person who operates in love every day of my life. I am patient, I am kind, I do not envy other people around me, I am humble and do not act full of pride or like I am better than someone else. I look to serve others, not to be served, and I rejoice at justice, truth, and righteousness, not at evil. I believe the best of every person (including myself), and I am filled with perseverance. I love others as Christ has loved me and has laid down His life for me.

(1 Corinthians 13:4–7; John 15:12–14)

Developing Patience

I trust in the Lord and wait patiently for Him because I know He hears me. He is faithful to bring an answer for my situation, to deliver me from all my enemies, to set my feet upon a rock and establish my steps. I will not cast away my confidence in Him or in doing the right things because I know I will receive the promises and the blessings of God.

(Psalm 40:1–3, Hebrews 10:35–36)

Living in Peace

I do not allow myself to get caught up in the cares of the world; instead I choose to let God's peace rule and reign in my heart and mind. I know when I pray in faith, with thanksgiving, God's perfect peace—which sometimes I cannot even explain—will settle in my heart and will actually guard my mind from worry. God promises to strengthen me and to give me His peace. *(Philippians 4:6–7)*

Accepting Supernatural Protection

I am made in God's likeness and image; He lives inside of me, and so nothing or no one can overcome me. He causes the enemies who try to rise up before me to be defeated right in front of me, and I will watch as they flee in seven different directions! I put on the whole armor of God so that I will be able to stand against the wiles of the devil. I stand with His truth as my belt, His righteousness as my breastplate, and I shoe my feet with the preparation of the Gospel of peace. I take up the shield of faith with which I am able to quench all the fiery darts of the enemy. I put on the helmet of salvation and the sword of the Spirit, which is the Word of God. Jesus has given me the authority over all the power of the devil and nothing shall by any means harm me. *(Genesis 1:26; Ephesians 6:13–17; Luke 10:19)*

Trusting in God's Provision

God is my Father, and He will always provide my every need. There is no lack for those who seek Him, and those who follow

His ways shall not lack any good thing. Jesus promised if I ask anything in His name, He will do it, and when I seek first His kingdom and His way of doing things, all my needs will be met exceedingly above all that I can ask or think, according to the power that works in me.

(Psalm 34:9–10; Matthew 6:33; John 14:14; Ephesians 3:20)

Growing Relationships

As iron sharpens iron, so do my friends sharpen me when I seek to build godly relationships. The key to my success in every area will depend upon the kind of people I allow myself to be intimately connected with, therefore, I will choose wise Christian faith-filled friends. I do not isolate myself from close relationships because this is foolish and every day I take steps to build and nourish the friends I have in my life.

(Proverbs 27:17; Proverbs 18:1; Proverbs 13:20)

Framing Your Self-Image

I am made in the likeness and image of God and I was created to have dominion over everything in the earth; God has put everything under my feet. He loves me unconditionally, and I am precious in His sight as His thoughts toward me are innumerable; if I could count them, they would outnumber the stars! Through Jesus, I have access to the Father in Heaven, and I am a child of God. I am holy and blameless and above reproach in His sight;

therefore, I can walk boldly into His presence and receive whatever I need from Him.

(Genesis 1:26; Psalm 8:6, 139:17–18; Ephesians 2:18–19; Colossians 1:22)

Using the Power of Speech

Today let the words of my mouth and the meditation of my heart be acceptable in the sight of the Lord. My words are gracious and full of wisdom. God has given me the ability to speak clearly and wisely in every season and in every situation, and every morning, my ear is tuned in to His voice. Life and death are in the power of my tongue, so I choose carefully what I say each day.

(Psalm 19:14, 37:30; Proverbs 18:21; Isaiah 50:4)

Building Strength

God is my strength, my fortress, and my deliverer, He is the strength of my life; of whom should I be afraid? He gives power to the weak, and to those who have no might, He increases their strength. When I wait upon Him, and draw upon His strength within me, I will mount up with wings like eagles and I will run and not be weary; I will walk and not faint. God is able to make all grace abound toward me so that I will always have complete sufficiency in all things and have abundance for every good work. Even when I feel weak, I can be strong in His strength because the power of Christ rests upon me. I can do all things through Christ who strengthens me.

(Psalm 27:1; Isaiah 40:28–31; 2 Corinthians 9:8, 12:10; Philippians 4:13)

Overcoming Worry

I do not worry or have any anxiety about anything, but in everything, I pray my specific needs to God. Then I trust He has heard me, and I give thanks to Him by faith that He has answered my prayers. I allow His peace that passes my understanding to guard my heart and my mind. I focus my mind now on whatever is true, noble, just, pure, lovely, and of good report. I meditate on these things, not on the negativity from the input of the world. *(Philippians 4:6–8)*

VISION ▪

6 | What You See Is What You Get

Everyone around me was cheering and tossing up their graduation caps. After a speech from the valedictorian about how today was the first day of the rest of our lives, the band began to play and all the young men and women of Bethel High School's graduating class of 1973 were ready to celebrate. Well, almost all of them . . . I certainly was not. I remember this day so clearly because while everyone else was expressing how excited they were to go on to the next place in life, I felt completely empty. They were calling this the best day of their lives, but I wanted to say it was the scariest and worst day of my life. They saw this day as a beginning, and I could only see it as an end. I had no vision.

Remember back in the day when TV was not 24/7? I'm really going to show my age here, but for all of you young people reading this book, there was a time when the television channels did not broadcast around the clock and they would actually go off the air. Programming would end around midnight, footage of an American flag would wave while a sound track of a band performing the national anthem played, and then the screen would go to "white snow" and the sound would simply become static. There were no options to turn to because every single channel did the same thing. No matter which station you turned to, all you'd get was static.

This is kind of how I felt on the day I graduated high school. The structure of daily classes, the natural advancement to a higher grade, and the umbrella of security all this provided were now suddenly gone. Before, when I looked into my future, there was at least another grade level to shoot for, but now all of that had come to an end, and when I looked into my future the only thing I could picture was static. The band had played, the flag had flown, and now I was out of options. No matter where I turned to look into the future of my life, all I saw was static.

That evening, I tried to drown myself in a binge of alcohol and drugs, hoping to numb the fear and emptiness I felt inside. I don't remember much of the next few days, and it was at this point where everything in my life took a drastic turn for the worse. The next several months were filled with partying, car accidents, arrests, and convictions. Thank God, I did not kill myself before I had the opportunity to meet Julius Young, the man I mentioned at the beginning of this book, who became my spiritual father and mentor during this crucial time in my life. Through this relationship, I came to know Jesus Christ and began a journey of building a vision for my life that has formed me into the man I am today.

If you would have asked me the night of my graduation if I had a vision for my future, I assuredly would have answered, "No." However, the truth is I *did* have a vision. It wasn't what I wanted, but it was what I had. My vision for my life was failure, divorce, drugs, and depression. It's not a vision I set out purposefully to build for myself, but through the course of my life, it's what I drifted into. It's the kind of life I saw around me in my family and friends, and it's what I automatically assumed I would experience. I wasn't aware I had a choice in the matter, and I certainly had no clue I could change it.

Perhaps this is how you are feeling right now. You may not be experiencing as drastic a lifestyle as one that encompasses drug addictions and police custodies, but maybe you are unhappy with where you are today. Maybe you're in a job you dislike, or maybe your financial situation is far below what you want, or maybe your family life is suffering. Whatever the case may be, I want to encourage you: You *can* change whatever you do not like about your life right now into what you want it to be. It may take a little time, and it will take some work on your part, but if a convicted drug addict can do it, so can you! This transformation starts with faith—the first of "the 3"—and then is empowered by the second essential key to success: vision.

Everyone Has One

Every single person on this planet has a vision for his or her life. This is the single most important truth you must come to realize as you work to build the vision you want for your life. Whether or not you have purposed in your heart to frame a vision for your life, you have a vision, and it has nothing to do with what you want for your life. *Your vision is what you see and believe for your future.* When you close your eyes, it's the picture inside your heart that you truly believe you are moving toward. This vision could be good or it could be bad. It could be the exact opposite of what you desire for yourself, but nevertheless, whatever you secretly envision your life will become, so it will be.

Jesus tells us in Matthew 6:22–23, "The lamp of the body is the eye. If therefore your eye is good, your whole body will be full of light. But if your eye is bad, your whole body will be full of darkness. If therefore the light that is in you is darkness, how great is that darkness!" Obviously, Jesus isn't literally referring to your natural eyesight, because no matter how long you might look at the sun, the inside of your stomach is not going to become lit up. He's referring to your point of view, or how you see things. If you envision good things, and if you are focused on God's principles and promises, then your life will be lit up with His blessings. But if your point of view is negative, and if you are focused on what is ungodly and worldly, then your life will be dark—and *not* full of God's blessings.

Do you see the glass as half full or as half empty? When you look into your future, do you see opportunity, or can you only see the limits that hinder you? For instance, some people have a vision to be healthy and fit. They expect it for their lives, they believe they can achieve it, and so they act accordingly and move toward a life that is healthy and physically fit. Others have a vision to be unhealthy and unfit; they may hate it, they may want something completely different for their lives, but if it's what they truly believe is in their future, they will inevitably move toward obesity and disease.

What you see is what you get. In other words, where you are today, the life you are experiencing at this moment, is a direct result of your vision of yesterday, and what you truly believe about your life today is exactly where you will be in the future. You might be thinking, "Wait a minute, Pastor; this can't be right because I did *not* want to be here, and I don't like my life the way it is right now." Yes, this might be true, but for some reason you got here. It is because of the thoughts and beliefs in your heart and the subsequent actions you took throughout the course of your life up until now.

> In other words, where you are today, the life you are experiencing at this moment, is a direct result of your vision of yesterday, and what you truly believe about your life today is exactly where you will be in the future.

Most of us are like I was on my graduation day. We aren't aware we have a vision for our lives, and even if we are, we have no idea how to go about changing that vision. But do not get discouraged! As you read these next chapters, you will not only learn exactly what your vision is today, along with some insights on why you have that vision, but you will also be empowered with practical steps on how you can change that vision into anything you want it to be. In a later chapter in Matthew, Jesus is again teaching about how to live a God-centered life, and He says, "Either make the tree good and its fruit good, or else make the tree bad and its fruit bad; for a tree is known by its fruit" (Matthew 12:33). He gives us a vital key for a vision of success:

Make it good or make it bad. No matter what your "tree," or your life, is today, you can *make* it good!

The Accidental Tourist

There is a couple in our church, Paul and Debbie Willis, who have been leaders since the very beginning of the ministry and great friends to Wendy and me. A few years into the church, we all decided to take a vacation together. Neither of us had any children yet, so we had the luxury of going anywhere we wanted, for any length of time, without needing extensive planning. First, we rented a motor home and then we came up with the brilliant idea of just packing our bags and going wherever the spirit led us. We had no plan; we just turned the key and started driving... It was a terrible idea!

After the first miles of "Where do you want to go?" and "I don't know, where do *you* want to go?" we chose to drive to the coast. That took about three hours, and we stood and looked at the Pacific Ocean. Many of you probably have not been to the coast of western Washington; let's just say it's not nearly as magnificent as it can be hundreds of miles south. There are barely any waves, and when the tide is out, there can be a thick stench. Needless to say, it was a bit anticlimactic.

We grabbed a quick bite and then decided to take our haphazard adventure north. What if we drove to the farthest northwestern tip of the continental United States? Surely there must be a monument of Lewis and Clark or historic totem poles or something of the sort, right? So we began our trip to a place called Cape Flattery, near Neah Bay. We drove and we drove. As we did, the towns slowly began to shrink in size, and the roads began to shrink in size, until we found ourselves on an old, gravel logging road. One would think we would have turned around at that point, but we didn't have a vision to go anywhere else, so we thought we might as well keep going the way we were already going.

After a very long time of swerving to miss enormous potholes and dust invading every nook and cranny of the motor home, we finally realized that there was nothing to see! We had devoted all day and much of the night to driving, had to set up camp along that dark and desolate logging road, and it was all for nothing! Granted, we did have nice talks and about a million rounds of cards, not to mention a charming night spent in the parking lot of a Dairy Queen on the way home. But this adventure certainly did not go down in our books as one of our favorite vacations. Because none of us had a clear plan for this trip, we got exactly what we envisioned: nothing. In that amount of time we could have driven to see the amazing sights and mountains of the Northwest, or we could have taken a trip to Disneyland, but instead, we had nothing to show for our journey. Our eyes were dim, and so was our vacation.

Many of us live our lives this way: just going with the flow and allowing life to happen to us. The visions we have for our lives are "accidental." We did not develop them on purpose; they just happened as a result of the

> Many of us live our lives this way: just going with the flow and allowing life to happen to us. The visions we have for our lives are "accidental."

circumstances we faced and the lifestyle in which we were raised. As a result, we have thoughts in the back of our minds of what we believe our future will be. We may not even be aware of all those thoughts, but they exist in our hearts and minds nonetheless. If we grew up in a home with happy parents and a prosperous life, our accidental vision is generally one of success and happiness, and we will naturally move toward that kind of life, but if we grew up in a home of divorce, or abuse, or poverty, our accidental vision is generally one that reflects that environment. While we may not want what our parents had, and we may not purposefully try to recreate the same experiences, if it's the only vision we have in our hearts, then we will inevitably move toward that kind of life.

The vision for your life encompasses so many areas. If the only examples you have of growing old are of people being very sickly for years and needing around-the-clock care, then unless you have diligently chosen to build new thoughts inside your heart, your accidental vision for aging is probably not very positive. Similarly, if the authority figures in your life were abusive and controlling, if you have not purposed to change your perspective about what you think is "normal," then you will naturally gravitate toward these kinds of relationships. If you grew up in a transient home, moving every few years, then unless you work to change your vision about relationships, you might find it difficult to establish long-term friends. Whatever the case may be, if you are not actively working to create the vision you truly want for your life, you will simply by accident reproduce the life and the environment you were raised in.

It is God's will, His *gift*, for us to establish our purpose in life, to get a detailed vision for our future, and to go for His abundant blessings. We were created in His likeness and His image, and we have the incredible ability to choose what we want for our lives and make it come to pass. Your eye is the lamp of your body, and what you see for your future is what you will get. Let's take an honest look at the vision we have in our hearts. Let's thank God for the areas in which we are experiencing happiness and success, and let's go about changing those areas in which we are not. Jesus promised all of us in John 10:10, "I have come that they may have and enjoy life, and have it in abundance (to the full, till it overflows)" (AMP). Let's not settle for anything less than this kind of life! Let's establish our lives with amazing and exciting vision.

7 Big Vision, Big Dreams

Vision is a life force. It is a spiritual power that gives us the ability to move forward in life, to rise to the next level, and most important, to receive the fullness of what God has for every one of us. In the King James Bible, Proverbs 29:18 reads, "Where there is no vision, the people perish." This is an amazing thought, if you will stop and meditate upon this. God is telling us the vision we have inside of us is the very essence of our lives; it determines the quality *and* the length of our time here on Earth.

The apostle Paul was an incredible man of vision. From the Holy Spirit, he received a vision to preach the gospel to the Gentiles and anyone else God placed in his path. He was fearless in his pursuit and nothing was going to stop him. At one time, the Jewish leaders from Jerusalem gathered forty men to try to kill him, but they were unsuccessful. Paul was the Rambo of his time! Even Satan sent a messenger to harass and to attempt to hinder Paul's ministry, but through it all he only grew stronger. Another time, a crowd attacked him, stoned him, carried him out of the city, and left him for dead. He arose from his deathlike state and immediately walked back into that city preaching the same gospel! The vision for his life was so powerful; it would not let him die. Nothing can stop a Christian with a God-given vision.

On the other hand, the ultimate expression of a person with no vision (or actually, it is more accurate to say, a person who is blind to their vision) is one who is suicidal. He thinks he has no purpose to live, he has no hope for his future, and he feels completely helpless to change it, so he desires to end his life. Where there is no vision, people perish. Sometimes it's a quick suicide, but for many others, they live on a slower, more passive-aggressive path to suicide. They feel no real purpose for their lives, so they have horrible eating and exercise habits, or they damage their bodies with excessive drugs, alcohol, and smoking. If we cannot envision a good life, a prosperous life, a fulfilling life, then we will die on the inside, and sooner or later our health will follow.

In the New King James Version, Proverbs 29:18 says, "Where there is no revelation, the people cast off restraint." In other words, when we do not have a revelation of God's Word and His will for our lives, we live careless lives. We don't understand the eternal purpose for our lives and so we live selfishly, excessively, and loosely. We have no discipline or direction. Our priorities get all messed up, we feel confused, and we run amok. Let's not run amok! Let's learn to release the intense power of vision in our lives. If we will build a good vision, we will have a good life. If we will establish a large and prosperous vision, we will experience a large and prosperous life.

In the last section, we learned about faith and how integral it must be in our lives. But without vision, faith will always be elusive. Hebrews 11:1 tells us, "Now faith is the substance of things hoped for, the evidence of things not seen." Faith is vision! It's seeing as reality dreams and hopes that have not yet been manifested in the natural realm. Vision and faith are dependent upon each other in order to produce results.

> Faith is vision! It's seeing as reality dreams and hopes that have not yet been manifested in the natural realm. Vision and faith are dependent upon each other in order to produce results.

Remember, what we see and what we truly believe is what we will get. And no matter how incredibly God wants to bless us, our vision will determine what we will actually receive.

Psalm 78:41 says, "Yes, again and again they tempted God, and limited the Holy One of Israel." Because the Israelites forgot all God had done for them—how He had rescued them from slavery in Egypt, miraculously parted the Red Sea for them to flee to safety, and how He had supernaturally provided for them their food and shelter—they *limited* God. He was unable to bless them and provide the abundance He desired for them because their vision had shrunk down to minuscule proportions. They could have been living in a land flowing with milk and honey, and instead they were wandering around a mountain in a hot and dry desert, with no Starbucks in sight.

Is your vision limiting what God wants to do in your life?

When you close your eyes, do you see a prosperous you? An over-coming you? Is your vision such a driving force in your life that, like the apostle Paul, it could even prolong your life?

Pluck It Out

In Matthew 5:29, Jesus makes a striking remark: "If your right eye causes you to sin, pluck it out and cast it from you; for it is more profitable for you that one of your members perish, than for your whole body to be cast into hell." What in the world was Jesus talking about here?

Luckily for us, Jesus was not speaking literally; otherwise most of us would look like we just stepped off the production set of a pirate movie. He's not talking about our physical eye, because our physical eye does not directly cause us to sin. He's referring to the way we see life. If our attitude, our outlook, and the things we see in our future cause us to compromise, to quit, or to sin, we need to change it. In addition, if the things we are focused on, even in the natural sense, cause us to draw back, to think negatively, to shrink our visions, then we need to change those things, too. Jesus is trying to help us to understand the vital importance of our vision, and what we are seeing in both the natural realm and the spiritual realm. Our eyes are controlling our lives.

The enemy, who is the devil, understands this. He knows if he can keep us focused on our failures, our mistakes, on our pasts, and on anything else that is negative, he can hinder our lives. He is fully aware of the principles of God, and knows what people are consistently seeing is exactly what their futures will produce. So he works overtime to fill you with negative images, to bombard you with everything that's bad, and to keep your mind preoccupied by the mess of the world. We can see a perfect example of this in the book of Job.

In the Old Testament, there is the story of a man named Job. He was a very prosperous businessman, with wealth and a full family, but somehow Satan got a hook into this man's vision, and very soon, Job tragically lost everything: his business, his wealth, and his family. While he was lying in his poverty, grief, and sickness, he began to question how this could have happened to him. In Job 3:25, he cried out, "For the thing I greatly feared has come upon me, and what I dreaded has happened to me."

At that moment, he unwittingly stumbled upon the truth of the matter. For a time, maybe many years, Job had been holding on to a strong fear that one day he would lose everything he had. And what he saw in his vision is what he actually made happen. Now before some of you start freaking out about some of the fears you have had, thinking they are all of a sudden going to start manifesting in your life, notice what Job said. He didn't say he had a little inkling of a fear that popped up every once in a while. He said the thing that he greatly feared and dreaded came upon him. This isn't a fleeting thought or a scary scenario that he entertained a few times. He *greatly* feared and dreaded it. Dread makes you think and focus your attention upon something over and over. He meditated upon it; he imagined the terrible scenarios repeatedly. They became his vision and what he truly believed would happen in his life—and so it did.

There is a good ending to Job's story, however. The entire

book of Job only spans a portion of Job's life, and once he repented and completely surrendered his life over to God, within just about nine months, everything started to turn around. He began to fully trust God and build his vision around that trust, and at the end of his life, he recovered everything: family, business, wealth, and relationships. In fact, in the last few verses of the book of Job, it tells us the Lord blessed Job with twice as much as he had before and lists an amazing collection of his wealth.

Too bad Job didn't "pluck out his eye," which was causing him to sin, to shrink back, and to compromise. If he had been able to recognize that even in his abundance he was expecting great catastrophe, he could have changed his outlook on life to something more positive. He would have been able to prevent the tremendous loss he experienced, and simply continued to move to a higher level in every area of his life, but his accidental vision had become so normal to him; he didn't even know he possessed such a negative one until it was too late.

All of us must get sincere about our vision and what we are truly focusing on. We need to get serious about the promises of God and make sure the ingredients of our visions are of those promises and not of the stuff of the world. Just like Job, it is possible to change and to see a future with God all over it and His will being done in our lives. Let's not wait until we are in a place of despair and destruction. Let's purposefully focus on our faith (instead of our fears) and learn to meditate on a vision of hope and prosperity.

Day and Night

Joshua is a much better example for us than Job. He is a man who was able to embrace the huge vision God had for the nation of Israel and to lead them into their Promised Land. It did not come without some work, however.

In the first chapter of the book of Joshua, we see God giving Joshua the mandate to lead His people after Moses had died. As we read what God specifically instructed Joshua, we can see he probably had a few fears and some self-doubt about his ability to become Moses' successor. In just a few verses, God repeats Himself three times commanding Joshua to not be afraid and to be strong and very courageous. Then God gives him the formula on how to accomplish that confidence: "This Book of the Law shall not depart from your mouth, but you shall meditate in it day and night, that you may observe to do according to all that is written in it. For then you will make your way prosperous, and then you will have good success" (Joshua 1:8).

God needed Joshua to walk in extreme authority and confidence as a leader, and He provided him the way to achieve it. He told Josh to keep the entirety of his focus on the promises and ways of God (after all, it was the people's refusal to do so forty years ago that caused them to be wandering aimlessly in this desert for so long). Joshua meditated on God's Word day and night, he spoke it out of his mouth every chance he got, and he envisioned his way to be full of prosperity and good success. How do I know Joshua heeded God's advice? Because we can see the fruit of it in his life.

In chapter 6, Joshua leads the people to cross the river Jordan, and they come up to the first city they are going to have to fight. It's Jericho, and it's a massively fortified city with strong inhabitants. It's the same city that caused the Israelites to run like grasshoppers four decades before. This city is ready to engage in battle. But God says to Joshua, "See, I have given Jericho into your hands, its king and the mighty men of valor" (Joshua 6:2).

Joshua could have said, "Are you crazy? Look at that big city and those big walls! They're so thick they're riding chariots around on top of them. We are just a band of desert gypsies— how are *we* going to defeat *them*?" But this kind of response did not even occur to Joshua. His vision would not allow it. He was so drenched in the confidence of God's Word that he was able to embrace the command immediately. He understood the importance of vision, and that if he simply "saw" the victory, he would be able to achieve it. And he did.

If we will keep our focus set on God and His Word, we will be able to achieve everything we know God has planned for us. *If* we will meditate on His blessings and His ways day in and day out, *then* we will make our way toward prosperity and we will experience success. But we must be consistent. We will not be able to build God's vision for our lives by thinking about it once a week while we are sitting in church. It's got to be something we do every single day of our lives, because every single day of our lives the world is coming at us through radio, television, billboards, newspapers,

> If we will keep our focus set on God and His Word, we will be able to achieve everything we know God has planned for us.

and magazines. We can be like Job and spend our days fearing and dreading negative circumstances and everything we don't want to happen, or we can be like Joshua and fill our minds each day with the good things of God's Word.

Every day I speak God's Word over my life, the very ones I have given you in the Faith Manual. Thousands and thousands of times I have gone to the Word to see my true self, to define my vision, and to encourage myself with faith to overcome my fears. I have built my vision around what the Word of God says, not the lies the enemy would try to make me believe. As a result, I have been able to experience a rich and fulfilled life, and my life is not even half over! You can do it, too. *Any* area of your life you are dissatisfied with, you can build a vision through God's Word and begin to move your life toward that vision, but first let's talk about a crucial component that will determine your ability to go for the destiny God has designed for you.

8 | Vision Killers

Wendy and I had seen many pictures of the famous Sistine Chapel, but it was not until we were actually walking through this amazing church ourselves that we realized no photograph could ever do it justice. The arches and the domes were so much larger than we had imagined, and we could never have anticipated how it would feel to look at some of the most famous artwork in the world. As I stood gazing up at the ceiling, I could not help but wonder how Michelangelo was able to complete the massive work of painting twelve thousand square feet of ceiling space in a matter of only four years. Talk about having a vision . . .

When an artist like Michelangelo is planning to create a masterpiece, I think it would be safe to assume he doesn't just whip out an 8½ × 11-inch piece of paper and start sketching. When a painter is looking to produce a work he is hoping will become significant, he looks for the perfect canvas. The quality of that material is of utmost importance, and he will wait until he is able to find a complete and whole canvas before he starts to express physically the creative vision he has in his mind. He understands no matter how vivid the vision, without a great canvas, the end result will be flawed.

Just as the result of the artwork depends upon a strong and high-quality canvas, so our vision is related to our heart. The determining factor of how much of our vision actually manifests in our lifetime is a whole and healthy heart. The book of Proverbs expresses it this way: "My son, attend to my words; consent and submit to my sayings. Let them not depart from your sight; keep them in the center of your heart, For they are life to those who find them, healing and health to all their flesh. *Keep and guard your heart with all vigilance and above all that you guard, for out of it springs the issues of life*" (Proverbs 4:20–23, AMP; emphasis added).

> The determining factor of how much of our vision actually manifests in our lifetime is a whole and healthy heart.

The Bible tells us to guard our hearts with all vigilance, and above *all* that we guard, because the heart is actually what births everything in our lives: emotional and physical health, finances, and relationships. In one translation, it says that out of the heart flow the "borders" of life. In other words, the borders of our lives—or the extent to which we see our visions come to pass—are dictated by the condition of our hearts. Our influence, our experiences, our possessions, our impact—are all determined by the quality and the health of our hearts. Just like the painter with the canvas, no matter how big of a vision we can imagine, if our hearts cannot contain it, we will not be able to achieve it.

This is why many Christians are living frustrated. They hear the message of faith, they begin to read and to speak God's blessings over their lives, they start to envision a life of abundance in every area, and then they cannot seem to make what they see in their minds happen in their lives. They feel like they're stuck in the mud with all the intention of going forward but without the ability to do so. It's all because they have overlooked one vital component of walking an extraordinary life with God: the wholeness of their hearts. What is the condition of your heart? What's going on inside your heart?

Spiritual Heart Attacks

One of the most common causes of death in America is heart disease. Because of poor health, poor eating and exercising habits, and the inability to handle the stresses of life, people's physical hearts become weak and sick. It's one of the biggest killers as this disease causes heart blockages, malfunctions, and attacks.

This is true in the spiritual realm, too: I call it spiritual heart disease, or SHD. Because of poor spiritual habits, avoidance of internal issues and stressors, and a tendency to harbor grudges rather than forgive, many Christians today suffer from SHD. It manifests in many different forms: negative-heart disease, small-heart disease, fearful-heart disease, broken-heart disease, and the result is a spiritual heart attack. SHD is one of the biggest killers of faith in the Body of Christ and is responsible for keeping us from the careers, the marriages and families, the incomes, and the opportunities God has designed for us. This should not be so! We have the life and the power of God residing within us; we should be experiencing—and exemplifying—the true joy and peace a whole and healthy heart provides.

> Jesus wants our hearts to be completely healed and made whole; it is the very next thing He is concerned about after salvation.

In Luke 4:18, Jesus said, "The Spirit of the Lord is upon Me, because He has anointed Me to preach the gospel to the poor; He has sent Me to heal the broken-hearted." Jesus wants our hearts to be completely healed and made whole; it is the very next thing He is concerned about after salvation. He knows when you have a whole heart you will see purpose, destiny, opportunity, and increase and will be able to live a life that impacts your world. If you have a whole heart, you seek after the things of God, you are ready to embrace the blessings of God, and out of that heart, you are able to bring forth God's plans and purposes for your life. On the other hand, a weak and wounded heart will only be able to bring forth a weak and wounded life.

Jesus talks again about the condition of our hearts in Matthew 15. The scribes and Pharisees were very religious people, walking around with closed and embittered hearts. They weren't looking for what God had for them (or seeing that God was standing right before them); they were looking to protect their turf. They weren't thinking about how they could grow spiritually; they were seeking for ways to defend their position and authority. In verse 2, they confront Jesus and ask Him why His disciples aren't following the proper traditions of washing their hands before eating their bread.

In the next few verses, Jesus begins to address their attitudes and their defensive ways of thinking. Finally, in verses 16–20, He says, "Are you still without understanding? Do you not yet understand that whatever enters the mouth goes into the stomach and is eliminated? But those things which proceed out of the mouth come from the heart, and they defile a man. For out of the heart proceed evil thoughts, murders, adultery, fornications, thefts, false witnesses, blasphemies. These are the things that defile a man. But to eat with unwashed hands does not defile a man."

Jesus was trying to get these men to understand that God does not care about tradition, religion, diet, or most of anything else the Jewish leaders of that time were focused upon. All of these things only serve to distract us from the real issues of the Kingdom of God. If the enemy can get us sidetracked by worrying about image, or about the way our denomination says Christianity should be done, or by judging anyone who is different from us, then we will forget about the condition of our hearts. Satan knows our hearts will decide our future, and he will do anything to try to cause a spiritual heart attack. Let's not give him any place in our hearts, and let's learn to detect the signs of SHD.

Symptoms of SHD

In the next chapter, I'm going to walk you through some powerful steps to getting your heart to a place of complete healing and wholeness, but before we get to the prescription, we need to take some time on the examining table. If you recognize yourself in any (or all) of the descriptions below, do not be discouraged. In the very next chapter, we'll talk about how to start the journey of healing the broken parts of your heart.

Here are some ways to identify the symptoms of a broken and diseased spiritual heart.

1. Your heart feels bruised. When you have a serious bruise, you tend to protect that area of your body. With even the slightest poke, you can feel sharp pains shooting throughout the entire area, so you do everything you can to keep it covered. This is the same way with a bruised heart. You're sensitive, you're defensive, and you get nervous around people because you don't want them to hurt you. Your heart has already been hurt enough; you don't need anyone new coming and poking around in there. You feel like you can't really do what you want to do in life because of the pain you feel on the inside.

Many of us have bruised hearts along with very valid reasons why we are hurting: the domineering spouse who tore you down; the bosses who belittled and ignored you; the parents who called you stupid and no good; the rape, the incest, or the physical and emotional abuse. Many of us were victims in a very unfortunate environment, and then many of us went on with life and made some terrible choices that only caused more bruising.

As long as your heart stays bruised, you will live your life small—even if you possess a big vision inside of you. Remember, your heart is the canvas upon which the vision of your life is painted. If it is ragged and torn, your vision will be, too. But the wonderful blessing of being a Christian is we have God's power within us to bring about the healing we need; all we need to do is embrace His promises.

2. Your heart is angry. Whenever something doesn't go quite the way you planned, you get mad. You're mad because you have the wrong job; you're mad because the person in front of you isn't going fast enough; you're mad because your pants didn't fit this morning; you're mad because you broke a nail. You try to manage your anger, to control your outbursts, and to be nice and sweet, but the moment something goes awry, you're yelling four-letter words and kicking the cat.

Probably the worst thing about losing your cool is how terrible you feel afterward. As soon as you simmer down, the guilt and condemnation begin to flood in, and you feel like a failure. You apologize for the millionth time to your spouse, or your kids, or the boss, or your friend, and you wonder if you will be able to ever get out of this crazy cycle.

You *can* stop reacting with anger if you will come to a place of realization that the problem lies within your heart. Remember we read in Proverbs 4:23 that all the issues of life spring forth from the heart. Yours is broken with anger, and unless you purposefully work to build new habits and thought patterns, you will never start to turn your life around toward a more peaceable existence. It's not everybody else's fault; it's not that anyone is out to get you; it's simply somewhere along the road of life you have been hurt and anger is the only way you know how to release it. Nothing is impossible for you when God is working through you. You *can* learn to live without anger.

3. Your heart is afraid. You're afraid of getting hurt. You're afraid of what people might say. You're up at night worrying about what might happen. Fear is a torment of the devil that tries to rob you of the joys from everyday life. When fear is always in your life, your heart is broken. You will pull back the borders of your life in order to avoid those things that you fear. Because of fear, so many people will not step out into the vision they have inside, and instead they settle for a mediocre life, experiencing only a shadow of what they know they could become.

According to 2 Timothy 1:7, "God did not give you a spirit of fear, but one of power, love, and a sound mind." If you are a Christian and you are united with Christ, you have the power within you to withstand the temptation to live in fear. Sometimes you need to grab hold of the Word of God and do whatever you know God wants you to do even if you are terrified! That is better than sitting on the sidelines of life waiting for the feelings of fear to subside. The only way to get rid of fear is to face it. I always say, "Fear pounded on the door, faith opened it—and nothing was there!" Fear is scared. If you will just stand up to it, it will flee from you.

If this is an area you struggle with, take some time to reread and reread again the first section on faith. Faith is the opposite of fear, and much, much more powerful.

4. Your heart is pessimistic. "That probably won't work." "It'll never happen." "I'd never be able to do that." "It works for them, but it would never work for me." Do you hear yourself saying these kinds of phrases? Do you see the world as good or as bad? In terms of how you embrace life, do you often see possibilities or impossibilities? Do you wake up in the morning and think, "Something good is going to happen to me today!" Or do you say with resignation, "Dear God, I wonder what's going to happen today..."

A pessimistic heart is a broken heart and will always find excuses about why life is so difficult and how things will never get better. You will never be able to live in the abundance God has provided for you if you are caught in these types of beliefs. *Everything* about a life with God is going from glory to glory and living from blessing to even more blessings. If you are a pessimist, how can you possibly receive His plans and purposes for you?

If you find you often tend to believe the negative, it's time to heal that broken heart. In addition, you've probably never allowed yourself to establish a positive and prosperous vision for your life. Remember, Jesus came so that we—and that includes *you*—would experience an abundant overflowing-with-blessings life (John 10:10). No matter how many years you have dwelt in pessimism, you *can* learn to be the one who sees the glass as half full.

God cares about the condition of our hearts. He is concerned about what is in and what is coming out of our hearts, because that determines the quality of our lives and our ability to see our visions come to pass. God is for you, and He wants you to succeed, maybe even more than you do. He needs His kids to be a reflection of His goodness, mercy, love, and prosperity so the world will be drawn to know Jesus. Let's get our hearts whole so we can be those bright lights shining in our neighborhoods, in our workplaces, and in our cities.

9 | The Reins of Vision

I grew up around horses. In fact, there is a picture of me at two years old sitting as happy and content as can be right underneath a full-grown horse! As teenagers, my brother, Dale, and I would compete in rodeos as a roping team, and we spent countless summer afternoons grooming and exercising our horses. There is nothing like the feeling of going at a full sprint in the saddle of a strong horse.

The very first thing anyone learns about handling a horse is you need to have the confidence to know you—*not* the animal—are in control. Horses are very intelligent and perceptive, and they can sense immediately if the person sitting on their backs is a skilled equestrian or is a novice rider. Wendy learned this concept firsthand when I took her home to meet my mother for the first time. My mom still lived in the same house: land, pastures, horses, and all.

I saddled up two horses, threw the bridles on, and mounted my horse. Wendy just stood there looking a bit confused, so I told her, "Come on! Just jump on." She still stood there, and answered, "Huh?"

I helped her get up on the horse, and I could tell she was a bit nervous about it.

"What do I do?" she asked.

"Take the reins, and tell the horse where you want him to go. Just guide him, and he will follow."

I realized this whole experience was new for her. While I had been around horses all of my life, Wendy had never ridden before, and the thought that a small human being could control such a strong animal was foreign to her. She wasn't sure the horse was going to obey her, and feeling her tentativeness, the horse agreed with her. I showed her how to lead the horse with the reins and with authority. Very soon, she began to relax and confidently take control of the animal. And I guess it worked and she had fun, because she married me!

Many people approach life like the inexperienced rider. They aren't sure what they should do, and they don't believe they are going to be able to control the horse once they get into the saddle. So they say "Giddy-up!" and then hang on to the saddle for dear life as they allow life to lead them as opposed to them leading life. But believe me, unless you make that horse go where you want it to go, it will take you where it wants to go. As soon as that horse realizes you've given up control you're in trouble, and it will immediately begin to take advantage of you.

So it is with the world in which we live. When the spirit of this world realizes you've given up control, that you've surrendered to circumstance, that you've surrendered to negativity, sickness, and poverty, and you've turned over the reins of control to whomever or whatever happens to walk into your life, the world will break you, buck you, and beat you down. Suddenly, you realize that fear is running you, anxiety is making your decisions, and negative people are controlling you.

You are a child of the Most High God. You are made in His likeness and His image. Fear, anxiety, and negativity should not be controlling factors. Take hold of the reins of your life! You can make your life go where you want it to go and refuse to give up control to anyone or anything else. How is this accomplished? You make sure to get your heart whole and healed. Remember, *all* the issues of your life spring forth from your heart, and the wholeness of it determines the quality of your life. With a whole (healthy and renewed) heart, you are able to take control of the reins of life and bring forth a successful, abundant, prosperous life. With a wounded and weak heart, you will not have the strength to endure the trials and tribulations that come your way.

The Overflow

Jesus was not very fond of religious people. In Matthew 12, Jesus delivers a man from demons and some of the Pharisees accuse Him of working under the power of Satan. Needless to say, Jesus addresses their disbelief. In verses 34–35, He says, "Brood of vipers! [I'm sure He meant that in the nicest way.] How can you, being evil, speak good things? For *out of the abundance of the heart* the mouth speaks. A good man out of the good treasure of his heart brings forth good things, and an evil man out of the evil treasure brings forth evil things" (emphasis added). Again, we can see, it's all about our hearts and what is flowing out of them.

What is the abundance of your heart? Everybody has some good in their hearts, and everybody has a bit of creativity in terms of a bright future. But what is the abundance? Everybody can be nice to people sometimes, but what is the abundance? Everybody can have a positive attitude sometimes, but what is the abundance? You see, the key is in the *abundance* of the heart; the kinds of things that spill out when we are not purposefully trying to be on our best behavior. What is the abundance of *your* heart?

This is a tricky thing to know because we all want to believe what we want to believe about ourselves, not necessarily what is the truth. We want to think we are optimistic people, we are faith-filled believers, and we are disciplined in all our behaviors, but are we? It's like the person who struggles with his weight. He says he doesn't eat very much, that he never finishes an entire meal, but the fact is he is grabbing a donut here and a caramel latte there, some potato chips here and a handful of chocolate-covered almonds there. When you ask him, "How's your diet?" he says, "I really don't eat very much and can't understand why the weight isn't coming off." If he could get a real picture of his diet, he'd see that his three meals a day and hundred-plus-calorie snacks in between were adding up to several thousand calories a day.

It's very difficult to see yourself accurately and to recognize the true abundance of your heart. You have to really want it and be willing to get brutally honest with yourself. But if you will humbly assess yourself, God will not only show you what the condition of your heart is, He will also give you the tools and the wisdom to discover the healing and strength needed to find healing. If you lie to yourself and never face the issues you carry around with you, then you will never be able to bring about change and recovery. But if you will have the courage to be honest about the abundance of your heart, you can do something about it! You can say, "Wow, I've been pessimistic. I've been angry, fearful, and hurt. But now I'm going after God's healing; I'm going to make the abundance of my heart godly and good, full of faith, prosperity, and love. I'm going to bring forth a better marriage, a better job, and a better life!"

> It's very difficult to see yourself accurately and to recognize the true abundance of your heart. You have to really want it and be willing to get brutally honest with yourself.

Sure, there will be bumps along the way, but as long as you have taken control of the reins of life, you will be able to overcome by steering your way through it. When disease comes along, you will rise above it. When discouragement comes, you will know how to pull yourself back up. When all the negative stuff that's in this world tries to defeat you, you will have the strength to face it and to win. In the last chapter, we talked about some of the symptoms of a hurt and bruised heart. Now let's talk about some practical ways to heal and to enlarge your heart, and to make the abundance of your heart godly.

The Cure

The Word of God. It's the only cure. Big shocker, eh? When you learn the Word of God, speak the Word of God, believe the Word of God, and build your life around the Word of God, your heart will become completely healed and whole. It takes time, but it is the only remedy that will work 100 percent of the time. Yes, 12-step programs can help, and hours of counseling can bring understanding, but at the end of the day, the Word of God is the only sure-fire remedy to healing a diseased spiritual heart.

The only way you can honestly assess the condition of your heart is through the Word of God. James 1:22–25 says, "But be doers of the word, and not hearers only, deceiving yourselves. For if anyone is a hearer of the word and not a doer, he is like a man observing his natural face in a mirror; for he observes himself, goes away, and immediately forgets what kind of man he was. But he who looks into the perfect law of liberty and continues in it, and is not a forgetful hearer but a doer of the work, this one will be blessed in what he does."

The Word is a perfect mirror into our hearts, and when we spend time searching to find ourselves in God's Word, He can reveal our strengths and weaknesses. We can come to understand what is making up the abundance of our hearts and begin to change the things we don't want. The Word is the only standard we can trust, because unlike the world, it will never change and it will always come through. It's not just letters on a page. It actually contains power to transform our lives and bring healing to our hearts. In Hebrews 4:12 Paul writes, "For the word of God is living and powerful, and sharper than any two-edged sword, piercing even to the division of soul and spirit, and of joints and marrow, and is a discerner of the thoughts and intents of the heart."

> The Word is a perfect mirror into our hearts, and when we spend time searching to find ourselves in God's Word, He can reveal our strengths and weaknesses.

If we will let it, the Word will get inside our hearts, pierce through all the hurt, the junk, the image, the fears, and all that we want others to think about us. It penetrates into our souls—the thoughts and intents of our hearts—and is the only thing that can really discern right from wrong, good from bad, what will help us and what will hurt us, what will lift us up and what will pull us down. As the Word sinks down and begins to saturate our hearts, our lives naturally become bigger, healthier, and more effective. The Word of God must become a priority in our lives.

Many of us want to hear God speaking to us each day, but we don't want to take the time to learn what He has already said. In addition, most of the time when God speaks to one of His kids, it actually is *through* His Word, as we are reading and studying our Bibles, and when His still, small voice does speak to our hearts, the message will always align with His Word. If we have not become familiar with the written Word, we may not recognize it as truth.

Spending time each day in God's Word does not have to become a heavy burden or an unrealistic goal you are attempting to achieve. It's simply about finding the routine that works best for you. Throughout my decades as a Christian, my life has moved through many seasons of change and likewise has my daily study of the Bible. Some years I have had the time to spend hours a day in the Word, and in others, not nearly that much. However, every day I have done *something*. Whether it's a teaching series from one of my favorite Bible teachers to listen to while I drive, or inspiring Word-based praise and worship on my iPod, I consistently find ways to put God's Word in my heart. At the very least, I read a proverb or a psalm, or I carry a card with a scripture on it that I can meditate upon throughout the day. Joshua 1:8 teaches, "This Book of the Law shall not depart from your mouth, but you shall meditate in it day and night, that you may observe to do according to all that is written in it. For then you will make your way prosperous, and then you will have good success."

Spend time in His Word. Even if it's only one scripture a day, if you meditate on it from morning until night, then by the end of the year, you will have come to know 365 truths! You will have planted 365 life-giving seeds into your heart that will each produce healing, strength, and prosperity in your life. When God's Word becomes more faithful and more real to us than anything else in this world, then we have opened up a pathway not only for God to speak freely into our lives but also for Him to bring us deep and complete healing in our hearts. And when our hearts are whole, vision and destiny will begin to spring forth like never before.

10 Vision Alignment

We all want to see our visions fulfilled. I don't believe any person truly desires to make it to the end of her life only to feel regret and disappointment about all the missed opportunities she passed up along the way. We are going for the bull's-eye for our lives. We want to be able to be like the apostle Paul and say, "I've fought the good fight of faith, and I've finished my course here on Earth." When we get to Heaven, we want to hear our Father say, "Well done, My good and faithful servant." The *last* thing we want to hear from Him is, "Well... you're done." Let's make sure we fulfill our visions.

Each of our lives consists of many parts: spiritual, physical, family and other relationships, and so on. All of these parts must be in alignment to experience the fulfillment of your vision.

The other day I was driving down a hill by my house, and

when I applied the brakes, my car started to vibrate. Immediately I knew what was wrong: My tires had gotten out of alignment. I must have bumped a curb or something that caused them to be tweaked off their normal rotation because I had not felt the vibration before that day. I also knew I needed to take my car in to the shop right away because if I kept driving with misaligned tires, something would end up breaking. Other parts of the car could become damaged and wear out before their time.

Alignment is also crucial in our bodies. If our spine gets out of alignment, we can definitely feel it. If there's a kink, or a vertebra is out of whack, then this will cause pain and limitations. We can't exercise like we want to, or play with the kids like we used to, because our backs are out of alignment, and until we make a visit to the chiropractor, we are uncomfortable. We don't sleep well, our bodies can get weak, and we become prone to sicknesses.

It's the same way with your life. In 1 Thessalonians 5:23, Paul writes, "Now may the God of peace Himself sanctify you completely [the old King James Version says "wholly"]; and may your whole spirit, soul, and body be preserved blameless at the coming of our Lord Jesus Christ." In order for your life to be complete and for you to see your vision fulfilled, your spirit, soul, body, and relationships must all be in alignment with that vision. Think of your vision as the body of a car and each of these components as one of the four wheels. If all are tracking and in alignment, then your vision will effortlessly speed along the road of destiny. But if any (or all) of them are out of whack, you are going to have a difficult time steering that car in the direction you want to go.

If you look at your life today and realize you are not experiencing the kind of success you want, it's probably because some aspect of your life is out of balance and alignment. If your marriage is not happy, or if your family is struggling, or if your business is not seeing increased profits, then ask yourself, "What's out of alignment? Where's the kink? What's causing the pain and limitation? Where's the problem that's keeping me from winning in this area?" Once you locate the issue and make the appropriate adjustments for realignment, you will begin to see your vision become a reality.

Aligning the Four Wheels

1. Your Spirit Romans 1:9 says, "God is my witness, Whom I serve with my spirit." Here, Paul is emphasizing that his spirit is involved with every part of his Christianity. He's not just trying out this Christian life, just going along to see if it all pans out. He's committed his spirit fully to the vision God placed within his heart. Likewise, your spirit must be aligned with your vision and vice versa. It is only through your spirit that God can speak to you and that the Holy Spirit can work through you.

Every day, engage your spirit with your vision so you can hear from God and know the steps He has ordered for you. You can do this by praying with the Holy Spirit, taking time to quiet your mind so you can sense how the Lord is leading you, and/or reading and studying the Bible. As you dedicate this spiritual time with God, He will show you how your business should grow, who to hire, and where to go in every decision. He will reveal to you the ways you can improve your marriage, how to parent your children, and who He has for you to be in relationship with. He'll lead you in your health, which supplements to take, and what kind of exercise is best for your body. God has more than enough wisdom for your every need, and when you seek after Him, and serve Him with your spirit, you will see clearly how to bring your vision to pass.

2. Your Soul Your mind, will, and emotions must be in alignment with your vision. This includes your desires, your knowledge, your education, and your actions. If someone says he has a vision to become an attorney, but he has not enrolled in law school, he's out of alignment. He doesn't really have a vision; he just has a fantasy or a nice idea. If he *really* had a vision, he'd get his soul educated.

By your actions, you can easily determine if your soul is aligned to your vision. Have you written your vision down? Habakkuk 2:2 says, "Then the Lord answered me and said: 'Write the vision and make it plain on tablets, that he may run who reads it.'" If you have never written your vision on a piece of paper, you do not own it and you haven't yet fully committed to it. If you cannot simply and concisely (don't write a book!) express the goals and the dreams you have for every area of your life, then all you have is a vague idea of a destination. Imagine if an archer's target was just a big red, blurry blob. How could he aim the arrow to hit the bull's-eye? When you write down your vision, you clarify it, you can locate the bull's-eye, and you can aim your life to hit the target dead center.

Another action that aligns your soul with your vision is your confession. Do you confess ownership of your vision, or do you just casually talk about it with your friends? Confessing ownership is not "I am thinking about starting a business." It's "I *am* starting a business; I *am* a business owner." The first is simply a fantasy, something you would like to accomplish some day; the second is a vision statement, something you have owned and are going to make happen. It's having the courage to speak out of your mouth the vision you know God has breathed in your heart. Never underestimate the importance of your confession. Remember, Proverbs 18:21 says, "Death and life are in the power of the tongue, and those who love it will eat its fruit." Every day, speak a bold confession of life about your vision.

Throughout the world, there are many people (and I'm talking about Christians, too) who exist in a place of soul misalignment and never even realize it. If you are driving to work and hating it, wishing you could be home with your kids, or wishing you were doing something else, then every day your soul is out of alignment with your vision. Your "car" is vibrating, you're wearing out parts, and you're getting ready to break. Then you wonder why you got fired, or why you never get that raise, or why you have headaches all the time. You are out of alignment.

James 1:8 teaches us that a double-minded man is unstable in all his ways. If you are always wishing you were someplace other than where you are today, then you are unstable and you will not be able to produce the life you truly desire. You cannot be thinking, *I hate my boss*, and serve him in an excellent manner. If you are constantly meditating upon how much you don't want to be working in that cubicle, then not only will you not produce your best results, you will also not be able to move to a higher level of life. Wherever you are today in your career or in your season of life, choose to love it and operate in the best of your ability. Get committed to what God has given you today, and He will continue to bless you, open doors for you, and give you favor with man, until you experience the fulfillment of your vision.

3. Your Body According to 1 Corinthians 3:16, "Your body is the temple of the Holy Spirit." Your body is your earth suit—what you need in order to function on this earth—and it's the temple within which you and the Lord dwell. It is essential that your body be aligned to your vision. If you say you have a vision to be in the Ironman triathlon, but you have difficulty getting out of your La-Z-Boy, then your body is out of alignment with your vision. If you say you want to live a long life, but you are not taking care of your physical body, then again, you are out of alignment. To be here on Earth for a long time, you must keep your body healthy and in shape.

I travel throughout the world, and I see a great many people who do not truly have a vision to see their own grandchildren. I'm not trying to sound harsh, but it's true. Their bodies are so far out of alignment, it's obvious they aren't going to be around for very long. The obesity, the chain smoking, the excessive alcohol consumption, or simple laziness are prevalent in their lives, and if a change does not occur, sickness and disease will take over their bodies. We need to ask ourselves if we honestly have a vision to possess a long and healthy life. Remember, if you discover you don't, it is not too late to change your vision!

Let's align our bodies with our visions so we can be on Earth 100, 110, or even 120 years. I want to see my grandkids *and* my great-grandkids so I can witness the prosperity and wisdom I was able to pass on to those generations. Let's you and I have a contest to see who can live the most years on the planet. Then, whenever you want to smoke that Marlboro, you'll think, "Nah, that doesn't align with the vision I have for my life." Whenever you think about supersizing your fast food, you'll think, "Wait a minute—this isn't going to get me where I want to go. I think I'll order the salad instead." When we have a clear vision of a long and healthy future, it won't be hard to make the kinds of decisions that help our bodies bring that vision to fulfillment.

4. Your Relationships This one is the most important, because the people you decide to partner with in life will absolutely determine the level of success you will experience. Your relationships include your marriage, family, and your friends. It is vital for every one of us to ask, "Are my relationships in alignment with my vision?" Psalm 1:1–3 reads:

> *Blessed is the man*
> *Who walks not in the counsel of the ungodly,*
> *Nor stands in the path of sinners,*
> *Nor sits in the seat of the scornful;*
> *But his delight is in the law of the LORD,*
> *And in His law he meditates day and night.*
> *He shall be like a tree*
> *Planted by the rivers of water,*
> *That brings forth its fruit in its season,*
> *Whose leaf also shall not wither;*
> *And whatever he does shall prosper.*

"*Whatever* he does shall prosper"! Are your relationships causing you to prosper? Who do you stand with? Who do you sit with? Who do you share your dreams and desires with? Jesus was very careful about who He spent time with and who He allowed to know His most intimate thoughts. He made sure his relationships were in alignment with His vision. We must do the same.

First, never talk about your vision to people who are incapable of embracing the full extent of your dream. These people can bring discouragement, talk about all the reasons why it won't work, and sow seeds of doubt in your heart. If you continue walking arm in arm with these types of people, you will eventually shrink your vision down to what they believe you can handle, rather than what *God* believes you can handle. You'll settle for a mediocre life and experience only a shadow of your original vision.

Instead, discuss your vision with faith people—people who know the Word of God, who live the Word, and who are growing and changing according to the Word. These are the kinds of people who will be able to agree with your vision, who will encourage you to go for your destiny, and maybe even challenge you to dream bigger. In addition, as you talk with these friends, your vision will become clearer in your own heart and mind. When you talk through the dreams God has placed in your heart, it's like focusing the lens on a camera. The more you share, what might have started out as a foggy or vague idea will soon become an outline and will eventually transform into a sharp, full-color picture. Proverbs 11:14 says, "Where there is no counsel, the people fall; but in the multitude of counselors there is safety." As they give their input and add their faith to yours, you will continue to clarify and put that vision into life.

Second, find a role model. In Matthew 4:19, Jesus told the disciples, "Follow me, and I will make you fishers of men." He knew if these men would live with him, travel with him, and do ministry with him, they would soon be able to become like Him. Then in 1 Corinthians 4:17, the apostle Paul told Timothy to follow him as he followed Christ. Paul understood all Christians would need an example, someone to look to as a role model, and who could help them learn how to become happy, successful Christians. He encouraged Timothy to be an example for the believers in his sphere of influence (1 Timothy 4:12) so they would know how to develop and to live their lives.

In whatever area you are growing your vision, look for an example to follow. If you are a young mother, find a wise older woman who has raised successful children or who is in the process of building a family that appears happy and positive. Learn from her; ask her questions; allow her to speak into your life. If you are a businessperson, find a role model who is experiencing prosperity in your field. How does he negotiate? How does he lead his staff? How does he make decisions? If you will do what he is doing, you will also prosper. I'm not suggesting you just copy or emulate someone; you have to stay true to your own personality and to your own specifics as God has given you, but you will be able to learn and glean from someone else's example.

When Wendy and I were expecting our first child, Caleb, I realized I needed some practical experience, so I volunteered in the day care we had at the church. I went in to learn how to change diapers and various other things related to caring for an infant. I wanted to learn to handle a baby safely. We took a course in parenting and as our kids were growing we asked for advice from successful parents as to how to handle certain situations and gleaned knowledge from them.

A good father can help you understand how to become a good father. Likewise, a prosperous woman can show you how to become prosperous. A great teacher can help you become an influential instructor. Get a picture and a strong role model, and you will be able to stand on their shoulders as you go for your vision.

Take some time to ensure every area of your life is in alignment with the vision God has given you. If you find one of your wheels is a bit wobbly, then get out your tools and straighten it. Don't ignore the vibrations warning you that something in your life might be out of balance, because if you keep driving forward in misalignment, there's eventually going to be a breakdown. God is committed to you for the long haul, and He's ready to bless you beyond what you could ever ask or imagine, but you must be in alignment to be able to handle the journey.

Vision is the second of "the 3." Faith comes first, as without it an eternal vision is impossible, but the two are so intricately intertwined. Strong faith is great, focused vision is motivating, but it is only when the two intersect that we begin to operate in the supernatural. Again, my desire is not merely to give you scripture and stories about vision; I want to leave you with tools to build and to clarify a faith-filled vision for your life. The Vision Manual, which follows, will provide you a dynamic, step-by-step process that you can use to encourage yourself, focus your life, and enlarge your present vision and goals. Let's begin to see ourselves as the true world changers God created us to be!

VISION MANUAL

Vision

As we have read, every person has a specific destiny for his or her life, and it begins with the God-given vision within your heart. Right now, as you read this book, you may be feeling completely lost as far as the direction you need to take for your life. Or maybe you are at a crossroads, finishing a very productive season of your life but feeling that God now has something new for you to accomplish.

Many years ago, I was seeking God and asking Him how I could help people to understand not only how to discover the specifics of their destinies but also how to know which ways to go throughout the many seasons of their lives. I wanted to give people a resource that would help them to see their futures through God's eyes and to be confident their steps were indeed ordered by Him. As I studied, I wrote down ten questions I believe were

Holy Spirit–inspired. Not only have I taught these questions around the world and for many years, I have also used them as a guide in my own personal life of ministry. Whenever I am going through a major transition, or our ministry is on the brink of making important decisions, I have applied these ten questions to those situations in order to bring the needed clarity of vision for that next season.

Take time with this Vision Manual. Carefully read and meditate upon these ten questions. Just as they have operated as a guide for my life and the lives of countless others, I am certain God will speak to your heart and enable you to see your life through His eyes.

The 10 Key Questions to Help Discover Your Vision

1. What is the deepest desire of your heart?

"Delight yourself also in the Lord, and He shall give you the desires of your heart" (Psalm 37:4).

I see two truths in this verse: First, as I delight in knowing and serving God, He places desires within my heart. He knows the destiny for which He created me, the things that will give me the most joy and satisfaction, and He causes me to desire those things that are in His plan for my life. Second, as I delight in knowing and serving God, He gives the things I desire, and this is in *all* realms: spiritually, emotionally, relationally, physically, and financially. Just as a father on Earth desires to give good gifts to his children, so our Heavenly Father desires to give good gifts to His children.

Some religions try to teach us desires are wrong or evil and should be denied or suppressed. Many who were raised in church feel guilty for having desires and would never expect God to fulfill them, and unfortunately, this is one of the reasons why many people leave the church. They aren't able to deal with the conflict of having desires and feeling guilty about them.

Desire is not only God given, it is part of the development of destiny in our lives. It's the very thing that helps us focus our vision! The young man who loves to talk and always gets the teacher's note "talks too much in class" on his report cards may someday communicate truths that will change the lives of his listeners. The young woman who loves to tell everyone what to do and take control of every situation may someday lead a large company or help to govern the lives of people.

Once I had a conversation with a man in our church about the "evils" of desire. He had been raised in a church that taught whatever the things were that he desired were probably of the flesh or from the devil. Because of this, he was hesitant to give God the reins of his life. In fact, he thought the thing he really didn't want to do was probably what God was going to ask him to do. In his mind, his destiny was found in the thing he despised the most. By doing what he didn't really want to do, he felt he was being more "spiritual."

Dr. Fred Price once said, "It is hard enough for God to get people to be productive Christians by calling them to do what they truly desire. It would be next to impossible to get them to produce good fruit by doing things they don't desire." I've actually had people say to me, "I don't want to make Jesus Lord of my life because I'm afraid He might tell me to go become a missionary in Africa. I would hate that!"

God doesn't work that way. Desire is a God-given force that He uses to help us to focus His vision for our lives and to fulfill our destinies. I'm not saying we are under some form of control by God; He has given us a free will. However, God knows our personality, our gifts, and our talents. He uses those things and causes us to desire the experiences that offer great excitement, fulfillment, and satisfaction.

But what is a "desire"? We all have had whims, fantasies, and wishes throughout our lives. So many times, we mistake the passing fancies of our imaginations for God-given desires. For instance, the little boy who wants to be a baseball player, a fireman, and a policeman all in the same day is "trying on" his dreams and learning to distinguish his desires from his fantasies. As parents we can help him sort out all these things. For the Christian adult, the Holy Spirit will work inside our hearts and help us discern the difference between our true desires and our fantasies. Fantasies come and go, but desires last a lifetime.

The desire you feel to speak, to sing, to create, to manage, or to build is within you because God placed it there. As you separate your deep, heartfelt desires from your fantasies and ideas, you will naturally be drawn to study and prepare to do those things. Desire, as God created it, is a positive and very compelling motivation and can help you unlock the details of your vision. You will discover your destiny as you clarify the things you *really* want.

2. What stirs your passion?

Passion is the zeal, fire, excitement, and intensity you feel about things that are important to you. Passion is powerful. In John 2:15, there is an amazing account of how Jesus single-handedly cleansed the temple, Indiana Jones–style. With only a whip, He drove out the sellers of sacrificial animals, as well as the moneychangers, and He overturned their tables because they were turning something that was supposed to be holy into a means to make a greedy profit. Jesus was consumed with such a passion for the sacredness of the house of God he became violent. Later, the disciples remembered the verse from Psalm 69:9— "Zeal for Your house has eaten me up"—and they knew they had just witnessed this scripture come to life.

Passion stirs us to action; it causes us to *do* something. A passion for song, praise, and worship motivates us to learn, practice, and bring forth the music God has put in our hearts. A passion for children motivates us to reach out to young ones and to bring them up in the nurturing and admonishing teachings of the Lord. A passion for building stirs us to be concerned with the smallest detail of construction, making sure everything is done perfectly. A passion for numbers may lead us to accounting. A passion for words inspires us to write. A passion for helping others makes us decide to become nurses, social workers, or counselors.

One of the ways we can confirm the vision in our hearts is by answering the question "What makes me the most upset?" If we care to the point of anger about something, it may be a part of our heart. Sometimes we see issues that we couldn't care less about, but the person next to us is livid over them; other times we encounter situations and cannot understand why everyone is not as stirred up about them as we are. It all comes down to your passion.

Many great enterprises, businesses, ministries, schools, and movements have been started because of someone's anger. The late Lester Sumrall's Feed the Hungry program took root when he thought about God's people praying "Give us this day our daily bread" while many millions still suffered from hunger. This image would not leave his mind, and his compassion and pain drove him to this destiny.

Schools have been founded by teachers who could not stand the plight of underprivileged children. Businesses have been launched because someone was frustrated by inferior service from existing companies. All these things show the power of passion.

There is *something* that stirs your passion. Is it a desire to see the office work done more efficiently? To have people communicating more clearly? To hear truth being taught? To change a part of your city or government? The desires of your heart offer clues to the destiny for your life. *Discover your passion!* It runs through you like a stream. Perhaps now it is a small trickle, but with time, it can become a great river. What motivates you to do something, to actually get up off the couch and engage? What will you argue about, get stirred about, be upset about? This is a clue to your destiny.

3. What flows naturally out of you?

Your course of destiny will feel right and natural as you discover it. People who have identified their vision and have found their place in God's plan are doing what is natural to them. Of course it is exciting, challenging, and inspiring, but there is also something natural about it. Walking your God-given course will be like striding in the pair of shoes that fits perfectly, sitting in the cozy chair that feels better than any other, or wearing your favorite jacket. It may be too big or too small for someone else, but to you it is just right.

Sometimes this feeling that everything is just coming too easily is the very issue that keeps people from recognizing their gifts. They keep looking for something special, something unique and out of the ordinary, so they overlook the things they do best and avoid the things that come naturally. They keep trying to come up with something difficult.

I went to Bible school with a man named Terry Tarsiuk, and he became one of my best friends and a fellow minister. At that time, his vision was to become a pastor, and he tried for years to become a pastor and to start his own church. We had trained together for that purpose, and we both set out to make it happen. However, Terry was an amazing pianist and songwriter, and I always wondered why he didn't develop that area of ministry further. Several years after college, Terry came to be a part of Christian Faith Center as he prepared to start a church in Canada. After some time, he became a leader in our music ministry and had a profound impact on our church. Finally, his wife and others began to challenge him about what he was really called to do. We all sensed the great impact his music ministry was having on people, but he didn't see it.

From Terry's perspective, music was too easy. He'd played the piano all his life, and his musicality flowed so freely from him that he couldn't see just how unique his gift truly was. It took a little while, but finally he began to feel a sense of destiny about it. He realized everything he really wanted to give to people was happening via his music ministry; he didn't need to start a church. In fact, many aspects of pastoring weren't even exciting or interesting to him. He soon changed his course, refocused his vision, and became part of our leadership team. After almost thirty years, Terry's ministry has touched thousands of people and he is a great blessing around the world.

Terry almost missed his God-given destiny because he was so close to it; it felt too natural and normal to him. He had grown up knowing he was called to the ministry, and to him that meant he was to be a pastor. As a result, this was the direction he was heading, but God had called him to be something else. When you hear Terry tell of this process today, you'll hear him thank God (and his wife) for helping him plug into his real destiny. Pastoring would not have been successful for him—at least not as successful as his music ministry is now. Terry is now using his gifts and performing the function for which he was designed. He is living out his destiny!

Romans 12:4–6 says, "For as we have many members in one body, but all the members do not have the same function, so we, being many, are one body in Christ, and individually members of one another. Having then gifts differing according to the grace that is given to us, let us use them."

God has given you grace to do what He has gifted you to do. With that gift, comes grace. Whatever part of His body you are, your function will flow naturally, because you have the grace for it.

Your feet are designed to keep the body upright and to walk, run, and dance; they have what it takes to do their job without difficulty. You can walk on your hands and knees, but it isn't natural, efficient, or comfortable. Your hands don't have the grace for walking, but your feet do. Every part of your physical body has a natural function. Similarly, you are a part of the body of Christ. There is a place where you will function in the church and the world without strain. You have the grace and the gifts to get the job done. Not that you don't have to work and apply yourself, but there will be a natural feeling about what you are doing.

Teaching, preaching, working with leaders, managing money, and building new buildings feel so good to me because they are all part of my function. People have asked me, "Aren't you going crazy with all these activities? How do you handle the pressure?" To me it is not pressure; it is a joy. I have the grace and the gifts to perform my duties as a pastor because this is my destiny. *Your* calling is the specific thing you do—a career or job or ministry in which God has placed you as you seek to accomplish a purpose, fulfill a vision, and complete your course of destiny.

A teacher can handle twenty-five active minds and bodies, the builder can decipher complex blueprints, and the salesman can handle the resistant customers because that is their calling. It is their destiny!

Find what flows naturally—what feels normal. This is likely your calling on the road of destiny. It may be big or small; the size of the task doesn't matter. You may think it's easy, but to others it would be difficult. If the shoe fits, wear it, and stop looking for your destiny in the wrong places.

4. Where do you bring forth fruit or produce good results?

"A tree is known by its fruit" (Matthew 12:33). If it's God's plan, a tree will be fruitful.

Jesus told a parable of an orchard with a fig tree that wasn't bearing any fruit (Luke 13:6–9). The owner gave the orchard keeper one year to make it productive. If it didn't bring forth fruit, he said, "Cut it down—what use is it to just take up the ground?" God isn't interested in things that don't work and are not producing any results. If you've been leading a church for ten years and have twenty-five people, I'd say you are not living your destiny—unless, of course, you live in a town with a population of fifty.

If your business hasn't made a profit in a very long time, then it's time to "fertilize" that tree and make whatever adjustments are appropriate to turn that thing around. But if you keep going backward year after year, then shut that business down and get on to something more productive. Look deep within to uncover the true vision in your heart. Too many Christians are wasting their time (and talents) trying to do things that for them are irrelevant and unproductive. You owe it to yourself and your Lord to be fruitful.

The exciting thing about your vision and your destiny is the Bible tells us we were designed in the counsel of God's will (Ephesians 1:11). He created you for a very specific purpose. God had a person or people He needed to affect in the world in some way—and so you were born. It's not that you were born and then God came up with something for you to do. It's the exact opposite: God had something for you to do *before* the foundation of the

world, and you were born to do it! Your purpose was established—
then your existence was established. God has a productive and
prosperous life planned for you, a life of meaning and purpose
that will make a difference in the lives of others and in His Kingdom. It may be to affect one person or family who then go on to
affect many others. It may be to raise great kids and then help
other parents do the same (what a tremendous need *that* is in
today's world). It may be to assist someone who is touching other
lives and to help make that ministry or business a success.

God wants every person to do the following:

- Live a long, healthy life (Psalm 91:16).

- Have a good marriage and family relationships (Genesis
  1:28; 2:18).

- Show financial generosity (Proverbs 3:9–10).

- Be a positive influence on other people (Matthew 22:39).

One thing you should know for sure: God has not planned a
barely get by, mediocre, mundane life for you. It is not part of
God's character to bring someone into the world for no purpose,
or even for a minimal purpose. In addition, He has never created
anyone for an evil purpose or just so that bad things could happen to them. Yes, there are times of struggle and despair in every
life. There are times of sowing and times of reaping. We all go
through winters before we enjoy the summer, but God planned
for every one of us to bring forth good fruit throughout our lifetime. God is a good shepherd, not an evil one, and if we walk
with Him we shall not lack any good thing. There will be times

we will go through valleys—even the valley of the shadow of death, but He will never leave us there to camp in the valley. With Jesus, we will always go through it to reach our destiny.

5. What is the witness of the Holy Spirit in your spirit?

"For as many as are led by the Spirit of God, these are sons of God ... The Spirit Himself bears witness with our spirit that we are children of God" (Romans 8:14, 16).

God has a way of letting us know what is right, what is wrong, and what His will is. Call it a feeling, a knowing, an intuition, or a green light on the inside; we all have a witness in our spirit when something is in question. Sometimes we get a sense about a certain circumstance and we just know that person is not telling us the full truth or is trying to hide something. Other times, we feel an inclination about particular opportunities and whether or not we should embrace them or let them go.

This is not usually an audible voice; it's just a witness in our heart. It's a spiritual directive about what we should or should not do. Even people who don't know God have some ability to discern His desires for their lives; but for the Christian, the Holy Spirit lives inside of each one to tell us what to do. How amazing is it that God Himself, in all His infinite wisdom, lives on the inside of us and directs and guides us?

Sure, there are times when we "miss it," when we either misunderstand God's direction or ignore it altogether. We are human and make mistakes, but as we grow and mature in our relationship with the Lord, and become more sensitive to His promptings inside of us, His voice gets clearer, and we can sense more clearly what to do.

It's like developing an ear for music. When listening to a song, most people hear only a small portion of the sounds and arrangements. They listen to the words and may even hear one or two specific instruments. The fact is, there are dozens of sounds and layers in the production of most songs, and only the trained ear will be able to decipher all of them. A person with a career in music production can hear bass, percussion, strings, and vocals, all at the same time. He can tune his ears to move from layer to layer as the music progresses. So it is with the witness of the Spirit; with practice and focus in your inner being, you can learn to hear the voice of the Spirit—even when the sounds of the world seem to be drowning it out.

Sometimes the Spirit's directive may be contrary to what your reason tells you. Not that we are to turn off our brains, but there are times when God leads us in a direction that makes absolutely no sense to us at all. I remember a time when my congregation and I were faced with a decision about church facilities. This was a major decision, and several of the elders were nervous about it. After much prayer, discussion, and counsel from other leaders, it came down to decision time. All I had to go on was a witness of the Holy Spirit about what He wanted us to do. There were great arguments for and against the project. In addition, there were other options that seemed viable. In the end, I had to decide, and I went with the witness of the Spirit, not any other rationale. I'm so glad I did, because in the years following, we completed that project, and it wound up being very profitable for our ministry.

Follow the prompting of the Holy Spirit in your spirit. God's direction will help you to grab hold of and clearly focus the vision in your heart. Sometimes you won't be able to explain it; you will just know you are supposed to walk in a particular direction. You may make mistakes, but you'll pick yourself up and go again. God wants to direct your life by the Spirit within you. Let Him do it.

6. What do mature Christians see in you?

As you are growing in destiny and going after the life God has designed for you, it is important to remember, you are not alone. God will bring to you friends and leaders who can help you on to destiny's course. From their viewpoint, they will be able to see gifts and talents in you that you may have overlooked. They might be able to help you recognize situations you were going to pass up as incredible opportunities. In the journey of focusing our visions to be able to discern God's destiny for us, it is imperative we have mentors and friends who can help us along the way.

Proverbs 18:1 tells us, "A man who isolates himself seeks his own desire: He rages against all wise judgment."

Don't try to make every decision on your own. Use the gifts and talents of others. Although you cannot rely on them for any final decisions (you must be responsible for those), you can draw great wisdom and insight from them. Remember, we are the body of Christ. No member of our body functions completely separately from the other members. Our eyes need the brain to do its job, and our hand needs the arm to do its job. We should not try to discern and fulfill our destiny alone. Granted, this sixth question is assuming you are an active member in a local church body and have taken the time to build relationships with strong Christian people. If you have not, find out today how you can become involved with a productive, Bible-centered local church.

I realize it feels vulnerable to build friendships, not to mention the time it takes to build the kind of trust required to feel comfortable enough to be honest and transparent, but God *never* intended any of us to live alone and isolated. He will not only give you the wisdom to know who He would have you connect with, He will also give you the courage to approach them. If right now, you feel you have no one to pray with, to be completely open with, or to seek counsel from, don't just sit around and feel like a victim. Take some action and decide it's time to reach out, extend trust to someone, and build new relationships.

"Where there is no counsel, the people fall; but in the multitude of counselors there is safety" (Proverbs 11:14).

We can't possibly make all the right decisions on our own. Even when it comes to raising kids or handling money, we need input from others. But we need to be sure we are seeking counsel from mature, Christian people. Your mama or your uncle Billy Bob's best friend may not be the best source for information. You must be careful about the selection of friends you have. (Notice I used the word *selection*. Yes, just because you are related to someone does not automatically give them the place to speak into your life.)

Take a good look at your closest friends, the ones with whom you share most of your life. Whether you realize it or not, you are becoming like them, and they like you. "He who walks with wise men will be wise; but the companion of fools will be destroyed"

(Proverbs 13:20). The more time you spend with an individual, the more like-minded you become with him or her. If your friends have a negative outlook on life, it will be very difficult for you to maintain a positive one. If they view themselves as victims, as strugglers, or as the ones who never have enough of anything, you will begin to think just like they do. If their marriages are bad, they may negatively impact yours. If they are always in a financial crisis, they may negatively affect your financial life. If they always struggle with their health, they may put doubts in your mind about your own health. Be very careful in whom you choose as your close friends, because "the companion of fools will be destroyed."

7. What career or ministry do you feel the peace of God about pursuing?

When we are on course with our God-given destiny, there will be a peace that passes understanding in our life. Even when this destiny takes us to extreme and challenging circumstances, we are able to rest in the knowledge we are smack-dab in the middle of God's plan for our lives. Philippians 4:6–7 says, "Be anxious for nothing, but in everything by prayer and supplication, with thanksgiving, let your requests be made known to God; and the peace of God, which surpasses all understanding, will guard your hearts and minds through Christ Jesus."

This kind of God-peace goes beyond the natural mind. It defies understanding or explanation. It is a supernatural part of knowing you are on course with God and with your destiny—convinced that before the foundation of the world, God established a destiny for you and that you are on your way to fulfilling it.

There have been several times throughout the history of Christian Faith Center when things were not easy. Financial needs, people problems, staff changes, and personal doubts are just a few of the things that have caused me some frustration over these three decades of ministry. Nevertheless, after prayer, meditation, and discussion with friends, I always come back to God's peace that surpasses my understanding. I have a sense the way has been prepared for me, and even though the hill might get steep and long, I know I will make it. I will finish the course.

I'm convinced many of those who suffer from heart attacks, ulcers, headaches, high blood pressure, and other stress-related conditions, do not know this peace. They don't know or they doubt God's destiny for them, so they worry and wonder about all their decisions. As a result, they have no peace and soon lose control of their emotions, feelings, and health.

Paul told us that the peace of God would guard our hearts and our minds. The use of the word *guard* implies a garrison or protective force that stops the destructive forces of fear, anxiety, and confusion. "God has not given us a spirit of fear, but of power and of love and of a sound mind" (2 Timothy 1:7).

When we choose to walk in peace, everything in life becomes easier. We find the ability to love those who may try to use and abuse us; we are able to keep our hearts soft and free from bitterness. No matter what the challenge, the peace of God helps us to go home at night and not let the cares of the day intrude on our time with our spouse and children. And when problems arise, the peace of God keeps us from freaking out and getting off course. In His peace we just keep moving forward in destiny.

Isaiah 26:3 tells us, "You will keep him in perfect peace, whose mind is stayed on You, because he trusts in You." When we can clearly see God's vision for our lives, we trust Him to lead us day by day and to help us reach our goals. We can be at perfect peace, and our minds will be clear and focused. However, if we focus on the troubles, fears, and worries of life, we'll quickly lose the peace of God.

Colossians 3:15 says, "And let the peace of God rule in your hearts, to which also you were called in one body; and be thankful." The Amplified Bible says to let the peace of God be the "umpire of your life." Imagine what would happen if the athletes were left to make their own decisions on a playing field! The pitcher would never agree with the batter, basketball players would kill each other over foul decisions, and as far as rugby goes, well, let's not even go there. Umpires and referees bring order and discipline to whatever sport they are officiating in. They decide what is fair and what is foul, and they help to keep the games from ending in a standstill.

So it is with your life. As you find peace with God and man, you will find a place of strength and order. Confusion will keep to a minimum, and order will be present in your heart and mind. Disagreement with yourself will no longer drain your energy or restrict your vision.

Let God's peace call the balls and strikes in your path of destiny. Let it say whether a decision is safe or out of the question, and let it direct the game of life so you will stay in order and under control.

8. What thoughts, visions, or dreams are impossible to put out of your mind?

In Acts 2:17, we find the Holy Spirit was giving visions and dreams to all flesh, young and old. It seemed everyone was overflowing with ideas. We can be, too. The very same Holy Spirit residing in those first Christians is the same One who abides in every believer today—we simply need to be able to recognize it. Most of the time when the Lord plants something in our spirit, it becomes a thought or an idea that just won't go away. "The spirit of a man is the lamp of the Lord, searching all the inner depths of his heart" (Proverbs 20:27). It's as if God turns the light on inside us, and no matter how much we try, we can't extinguish it.

As a young Christian, I began to think about the ways in which I could help others and make a difference in their lives. At that point and with simply a genesis of an idea, I was already on the course of destiny, even though I didn't know much about what it was going to look like. My dream of helping others would not go away; in fact, it only increased as I matured in my relationship with Jesus. I could not reject or escape this vision because it stayed with me for years until it finally grew into a vision of Christian Faith Center.

What thoughts, visions, or ideas are swirling around inside of you? What are the true dreams (not just fantasies) you cannot seem to shake off? Many times we bury these visions under a pile of doubt, fear, and rationalizations for why it could never work, but if instead you decide to view your future through the eyes of faith, what ideas begin to emerge? Those thoughts and visions and dreams that stay with you may indicate God's plan for your destiny. Make sure you are not too quick to shove them off to the side.

9. What vision can you give 100 percent of yourself to for your entire life?

Whatever God planned for you will require *all* your gifts, talents, strengths, and emotions. He did not give you abilities only to ignore some of them in His destiny for you. "We also ought to lay down our lives for the brethren," says 1 John 3:16. God will ask us to give everything we have for the people we serve. Fulfilling the vision God has for your life will not be an easy, part-time job which you can cruise through half asleep. You will be stretched to the limit. You will use everything within you, and you will have to dig deeply to finish your course.

One of the greatest tragedies in our world today is the number of people who go to work every day but never use what is really in them. They drive down the freeway with their brain still asleep, and they float through the day just trying to get by. They feel they are successful if they can simply keep a job. That's called "making a living," and it is a low level of life. Dogs make a living trying to be man's best friend. Monkeys make a living finding bananas. You and I are called to live lives of abundance, blessing, and prosperity in every area. We were not put on this planet to just make a living.

If you are involved in a job or a ministry that is not utilizing all the gifts and talents God has given you, if you are not deeply challenged to accomplish your goals, and if at the end of the day you put your head on your pillow with a nagging feeling of dissatisfaction—God has more for you! If you will take the risk to look inside your heart and discover the visions He has placed within you, you will find a destiny beyond your wildest dreams.

10. What do people want to gather around and help you accomplish?

The final questions you should consider to discover your destiny are these: What do people want to help me do? When I set out to accomplish something, do I find it easy to motivate people to join in the effort? This may apply more to those in leadership, but I believe every person is a leader of some sort. No matter where we are in life, there are people around us we are influencing and making a difference in their lives. It is important we realize this so we can best be the ambassadors for Christ that God needs us to be.

In the book of Acts, Paul receives a vision and shares it with his ministry team. Notice their response: "Now after he had seen the vision, immediately we sought to go to Macedonia, concluding the Lord had called us to preach the gospel to them" (Acts 16:10).

Paul had the vision, but all of those with him immediately picked it up and were willing to go with it. This is the dynamic that happens when destiny is obvious. People sense the power of it and want to get involved. Churches, ministries, and businesses that are born of God attract people, and like a magnet, draw them to become involved with the vision. Departments in the church or businesses destined to prosper simply will attract the necessary people to make them succeed. When no one is interested and no one will get involved, it could be (though it is not always) because this is not part of a destiny.

RENEWAL

RENEWAL

11 | Renewing the Mind

was still the same. I thought that I would somehow feel completely different. I kept hearing phrases like "new life," "new person," and "new creation," so I naturally assumed that when I gave my heart to Jesus everything in my life would change. But leaving the church that night, I still felt like me. Although I could not deny I now sensed a new hope within me for my future, all other aspects of my life seemed about the same. I was still on very strict probation, still returning to a drug rehabilitation program, and still had the same insecurities I had when I entered the church service that evening. Yes, something was different on the inside, but in all other areas, I remained an unchanged Casey Treat.

I am grateful to have had Julius as a mentor and spiritual father during that time, leading me and helping me to sort out the next weeks and months that followed. He was able to explain to me what the new birth was—and what it was not. Perhaps if he had not influenced my life at such a crucial point, I would have become discouraged by the fact that so much of me was still the same. I might have gone back to my former way of living and Christianity would have become just another "been there, done that" experience. Although I was saved, it really wouldn't have made much of an impact upon my life here on Earth.

This disillusionment I felt when I first became born again affects many Christians today. They believe in Jesus, are assured of their eternal salvation, even go to church every week, but they are confused. They hear God is a God of prosperity and blessing, but they are not experiencing a prosperous or blessed life. They read the promises of healing and emotional freedom in the scriptures, but they are still living fearful, anxious, angry, or depressed lives. And when they look at some other Christians around them, they witness the same unhappiness, the same cheating and lying, and the same pain that is experienced by people in the world.

As Christians, the people on Earth who are united with Christ, we ought to be the ones always on top, having the best jobs; raising successful, confident children; living free from debt and diseases; and being examples for everyone to follow. So often, the world looks at us and thinks, *Those Christians' lives are no better than mine, so why should I want to be like them?* Our divorce rate is the same as theirs. For many, our debt-to-income ratios are the same, and often our quality of life is the same. How sad that we have the Spirit of the One who created the universe and the power of Jesus that reigns over death residing on the inside of us, and the world looks at us and wonders why so many of our lives are just as messy as theirs! How can this be? How is it possible for a person who has the King of kings and Lord of lords living on the inside of them to live a mediocre, unfulfilled life or, even worse, a life of habitual sin?

Just because we are saved does not guarantee we will have a successful life on Earth. It simply means we will spend our eternal life in the presence of God. In fact, there are many Christians who are on their way to Heaven, but their earthly lives are lived separated from a real relationship with God. They exclude God and His ways from their finances, their marriages, and their parenting by turning to the world and its ways to seek the answers to their problems. Even for those who are growing in the Word of God, when we spend large amounts of time watching television, or when we allow laziness, anger, fear, or any other fleshly behavior to dominate our lives, we have let the things of the world take up room in our hearts instead of God, and then we wonder why we are not discovering the level of life the Bible says is available to us.

> Just because we are saved does not guarantee we will have a successful life on Earth.

When we became born again, the transformation that happened on the inside was *instant*, as our spirits came alive to God. However, the new birth was simply the first step of faith in our walk with God. Our spirits became new, but now, if we want to live a dynamic, prosperous life on Earth, we must use our faith to create a vision for our lives. But it cannot stop there. That would be like having a treasure map in our hands but never actually utilizing it to lead us to the treasure. We can look at the details drawn on that map all we want, but unless we get off our rusty dusty and *do* something, *go* somewhere, the chest of gold will stay buried.

This brings us to the last of "the 3." In order to experience the full richness of life God has intended for us, we must commit ourselves to a daily path of *renewal*. We need to use our faith and our vision as tools to reprogram our minds that have been conformed to the world by secular school, media, and television. It is only by thinking like God thinks that Christians can find the complete freedom they desire.

"And do not be conformed to this world, but be transformed by the renewing of your mind, that you may prove what is that

> It is only by thinking like God thinks that Christians can find the complete freedom they desire.

good and acceptable and perfect will of God" (Romans 12:2). This scripture is the most life-changing scripture Julius helped me to understand, and it is the crux of the message God has placed in my heart to teach around the world. It is as much alive to me today, if not more, than the first day I heard it well over thirty years ago, and I believe it is the most important scripture in the Bible, second only to John 3:16. Once a person is born again, if he can understand and embrace this revelation, he will, just as the passage promises, begin to walk in the perfect will of God for his life. God's perfect will—isn't that what we all are looking for? Striving for?

At nineteen years of age, I began to realize the same patterns of thoughts that led me to a reckless life of drug abuse were still alive in my head even after I had received salvation. Unless I worked at changing and renewing these thoughts, Julius explained, while I might possess the strength to live clean for a while, it wouldn't be long before I was right back into the drug lifestyle. For the first time in my life, I felt the incredible power of knowing I could change. Every habit, every insecurity, every thought—I was sure I could change them all! I could decide what I wanted my life to become, and through the strength of God working within me, I could achieve it!

Change Is Possible

Every fall, I am always amazed as I watch the birds gather and fly south for the winter. How do thousands of birds find each other, organize themselves, and then cooperate with each other to get to their warmer climate before the first freeze? Many of us have a hard enough time getting our own families out of the door for church every week, let alone arriving at the service before it starts! But unlike humans, animals operate on instinct. They do what they do because that's how God made them, and they don't think outside that parameter. You won't find a bird deciding whether or not he feels like flying south. Even if he is bone tired, he simply cannot help himself; he *must* fly south— it's instinctive.

Genesis 1:26 tells of another species created by God, one living on an entirely different level than instinct-driven creatures. "Then God said, 'Let Us make man in Our image, according to Our likeness; let them have dominion over the fish of the sea, over the birds of the air, and over the cattle, over all the earth and over every creeping thing that creeps on the earth.'" God set humankind completely apart from the animal kingdom. Not only do we possess dominion over the animals, but we also have been uniquely given the miraculous ability to change. We can choose who we want to become, how we relate with people, what to do with our gifts, talents, and destinies. We choose to be happy or not, to be prosperous or not, to be healthy or not. We are not subject to the confines of instinct. We have the free will to grow, to dream, and to change. The success for every realm of our lives dwells within every one of us. We just have to choose to access it!

So many people are dissatisfied with their lives, but they are waiting for someone to rescue them or to improve their lives. They feel they are victims of their circumstances, helpless to get out of what they feel is their lot in life. They believe the government should do more to take care of them, or that God should come down and magically fix everything for them, or maybe even that the devil needs to be cast out from their crisis. Waiting around for someone else to bring about the needed change in their lives will only bring extreme disappointment, because first of all, that's never going to happen. Second, the change they desire can only happen from within each one of them. It starts with new thoughts, new beliefs, and new habits. It starts with renewing the mind.

Paul wrote in the book of Romans that it was necessary for every Christian to be transformed by the renewing of the mind. In the original Greek language, the word used for "transformed" is *metamorpho* and literally means to be changed completely.

What this scripture in Romans 12:2 is revealing to us is that once we have become Christians, although our spirits are united with Christ, every other part of growth begins with the transformation that happens when we renew our minds. The power of this passage is a revelation every Christian must understand in order to succeed in life. It reveals that not only do we have within us the ability to change and to choose God's perfect will for our lives, but exactly *how* to bring about that change. It can only come about by renewing the mind.

We all have areas we wish could be better: our marriage, our relationships, our finances, our parenting habits, our weight. Many of us get stuck in our pain and problems in life, and we don't like where we are, but we don't know how to get out of these negative, or even just mediocre, situations. You are *stuck* with only those things that you allow! You are made in God's image; you possess an enormous capacity to learn and to grow—and to change. *Change* is not a bad word. It's the key to your success in life, and when you decide to operate in the strength God gifted you with, you can transform *any* area of your life that you desire.

Renewing the mind simply means exchanging your thoughts of negativity, doubt, fear, anxiety, prejudice, greed, and any other worldly perspective for the thoughts of God. Isaiah 55:7–8 says, "Let the wicked forsake his way, And the unrighteous man his thoughts [or, as Paul said it, do not be conformed to the world]; Let him return to the Lord, And He will have mercy on him; And to our God, For He will abundantly pardon. 'For My thoughts are not your thoughts, Nor are your ways My ways,' says the Lord."

The world is negative, depressed, and ever looking to

highlight bad news. Rarely does a newspaper headline or a special edition on the evening news communicate a wonderful, positive event. But we tune in to the news anyway. The editors know that fear sells, so you hear, "Could your drinking water be causing cancer? Tune in at ten tonight!" Or "Are your children at risk of being abducted by aliens? Find out the surprising facts in our special report." Usually, these teasers are grossly exaggerated and the news brief is actually just a simple, run-of-the-mill story. But ordinary stories don't attract viewership. Consequently the producers invent scary headlines so people will tune in. Fear and negativity are the air the world breathes.

When we conform to the world's attitudes, and our thinking flows along the current of its depressive mind-sets, then we will never be able to experience God's good and perfect will for our lives. We think, *I can't . . . , I'll never be . . . , I can't help that . . . ,* and *I don't have enough . . .* We suffocate the dreams for our lives with our poverty attitudes, low self-esteem, and victim mentality. But God is showing us another option! He's providing a new path for us to choose, a way to work out the salvation of our souls.

According to Romans 12:2 and Isaiah 55:7–8, God is telling us to get out of our culture. It's weighing us down and making us believe we are far less than what He created us to be! His thoughts and ways are far above the world's but completely available to every believer. If you will think like He thinks, believe what He believes, and see like He sees, you will naturally gravitate toward a higher level of life. You will clearly envision the exciting life He has planned for you and you will find the ability to accomplish your dreams.

If we will embrace the challenge to renew our minds to God's thoughts and God's ways, we can experience the incredibly abundant life He planned for us. It doesn't happen instantly, and there's no magic prayer to pray, but most long-lasting results never come quickly or easily. Renewal is a process that matures throughout our journey of life with God, and the rewards of joy, strength, inner wholeness, prosperity, and peace are so worth the effort.

Renewal Is Not a Secret

There are many popular philosophies today that claim they hold the keys to a person's spiritual, emotional, relational, and financial success. Many authors collectively making billions of dollars through their books and accompanying teaching resources brag they have the secret of the universe: "If you will simply follow these five easy steps, order my latest DVD, and join my monthly e-mail blast, you, too, can find spiritual enlightenment!" Then depending upon what famous movie star, athlete, or talk show host endorses the product, more and more of the masses thoughtlessly believe it as truth; thus, a new spiritual movement is born. But as quickly as these new philosophies rise to popularity is as quickly as they fade into the past as people begin to realize they didn't transform their lives like they had hoped. While some success might have been apparent for a while, the emptiness deep within their hearts still was not satisfied. They begin to look for the next big wave.

Renewing the mind is not, and will never be, part of this transient wave. It's not mind over matter, it's not just thinking happy thoughts, and it's not the law of attraction. It's not even disciplining yourself to become aware of every negative thought and replace it with a positive one. It's so much more powerful than that. Renewing the mind is exchanging the thoughts you have learned from the world for the life-changing thoughts of the One who created the universe. It's not just deciding to believe in whatever wind of doctrine happens to be popular at the time.

> Renewing the mind is exchanging the thoughts you have learned from the world for the life-changing thoughts of the One who created the universe.

These are man-made principles and ultimately lifeless. Renewing the mind is choosing as truth the very Word of God, which is alive and powerful, and making His Word our way of thinking. Hebrews 4:12 declares, "For the word of God is living and powerful, and sharper than any two-edged sword, piercing even to the division of soul and spirit, and of joints and marrow, and is a discerner of the thoughts and intents of the heart."

There is amazing, life-changing power in God's Word, and when we begin to conform our way of thinking to the realities of His Word, everything that once seemed impossible by the standards of the world becomes possible! Those areas of our life that once weighed us down, that appeared hopeless to change, now begin to lift. The dreams and visions for our lives we saw as unattainable now are right before our eyes, ready for the taking! We rise above the limitations of the world and begin to experience a supernatural way of life. The opportunity to possess a life such as this is within the reach of every Christian. It takes new knowledge and new beliefs. It takes renewing the mind.

12 | The Age-Old Battle

I saw a commercial on TV the other day that was promoting the latest and greatest drug therapy for a better sex life. The images were of several couples, all happy and romantic, dancing and enjoying their marriages. The voiceover, however, was quite the opposite as it listed the many side effects for the drug: increased risk of heart attack, loss of hearing, nausea, vision changes, and possibly blindness. I laughed. So the guy will have a better sex life, but he might go blind and deaf while he's having a heart attack. Great. At least he'll have a smile on his face.

The gurus in the world do not know how to answer the problems so many are facing today. Their solution is simply to prescribe a new drug to numb the anger, the depression, and the pain. They are eager to promote the newest program to lose weight, manage your emotions, and fix your addictions. They are even referring to the natural process of aging as a disease and are offering various medications and procedures to fight the "disease of aging"! You take the drug, but then you need another drug to offset the side effects of the first drug, and when it's time for you to go off these drugs, you need a third drug to help you with the withdrawal symptoms of the other two drugs. When does it end?

As Christians, let's not go for the remedies the world has to offer. Instead, let's decide to pursue God's perfect will for our lives. Let's walk in His plan for our spirit, soul, and body so that we can enjoy all the pleasures of life, including a fulfilling marriage and sexual relationship, without the cost (physical and financial) of a dozen prescription drugs. Living in God's perfect will, as we have already discussed, begins with becoming born again. This moves us toward salvation and an eternity spent in the presence of Jesus. However, just because we now have an open relationship with God doesn't mean we will have success in life or that our day-to-day experiences will become any better. This requires the next step: using our faith and vision to renew our minds. It's a lifelong process that moves us toward His perfect and acceptable will for our lives here on Earth.

Flesh Versus Spirit

Have you ever been in a situation when you knew what the right and honorable thing to do was but instead you responded in exactly the opposite way? Every person alive (or who has ever lived since the beginning of time for that matter) has found themselves acting in a way contrary to what they believe. We're driving in to the office, and we think, *I'm not going to let the stress of work affect me today. I'm going to lead my staff with grace and kindness.* And then, the first moment someone makes a mistake, we're screaming our heads off. Or we pick up the phone to call a friend and we think, *I promised I would not say anything to anyone about Jane's personal problems, and I will not breathe a word of it to my friend.* The next thing we know, we're blabbering Jane's confidences to another person. Then we feel terrible for doing what we did and think, *Why did I do that?*

Paul gives us the answer in Romans 7:18–25. Even for the Christian there exists a war between the sin that resides in our flesh and the spirit that is born again: "For I know that in me (that is, in my flesh) nothing good dwells; for to will is present with me, but how to perform what is good I do not find. For the good that I will to do, I do not do; but the evil I will not to do, that I practice. Now if I do what I will not to do, it is no longer I who do it, but sin that dwells in me. I find then a law, that evil is present with me, the one who wills to do good. For I delight in the law of God according to the inward man. But I see another law in my members, warring against the law of my mind, and bringing me into captivity to the law of sin which is in my members. O wretched man that I am! Who will deliver me from this body of death? I thank God— through Jesus Christ our Lord! So then, with the mind I myself serve the law of God, but with the flesh the law of sin."

The battle every Christian must engage in daily is one with the flesh in one corner squaring off with the spirit in the other. Every human is composed of three entities: spirit, soul, and body (flesh). Our flesh, or our body, operates solely through our senses, what we taste, see, hear, smell, and touch. It is what makes us desire things like alcohol, drugs, pornography, adultery, and other types of destructive lusts or behaviors. On the other hand, our spirits are our life force, and the moment we choose to believe in Jesus, our spirits become united with God. In this union of holiness, our spirits now only desire those things that bring life, joy, and peace. The flesh and the spirit stand contrary to each other, unable and unwilling to compromise. This standstill brings us to the deciding factor, the third entity of our triune being: the soul. The soul casts the swing vote, the one that determines the outcome of this war. If our soul votes for the flesh, we choose to live in the realm of our senses. If our soul votes for the spirit, we open up our lives to experience the realm of faith.

> The battle every Christian must engage in daily is one with the flesh in one corner squaring off with the spirit in the other.

Our soul also has three ingredients: our mind and how we think, our will and what we desire, and our emotions and how we feel about every aspect of our lives. The mind is the leader of the three, and where it goes, the will and the emotions will follow. Can you see why it is so important to renew our minds and learn how to think according to God's Word? If we want to win the war between the spirit and the flesh, we must sharpen our most vital weapon—our minds.

Every one of us has a body of flesh, and no matter how mature we become as Christians, this flesh will never stop trying to tempt us away from the things of God. At any point in our walk with God, if we become lazy in this fight, our flesh will take over.

In the Northwest, we have blackberry bushes that spring up everywhere. The branches are thick and thorny things and if not pruned back, they will spread fast and furious. At the beginning of spring, they look nice with their pretty white flowers, but if left to themselves, by the end of the summer you can lose your entire backyard to this bush. And once a blackberry bush has become overgrown, it takes a whole lot of work (and very thick gloves) to chop it down. The flesh is the same way. If we don't keep a close watch over it, it will try to take over our lives.

The incredible news is we have a choice! As Paul wrote, "Thank God, through Jesus Christ our Lord" we are not victims of our flesh (Romans 7:25). When we make the choice to renew our minds to God's Word, we move from the back of the car to the driver's seat, and we can steer the path of our decisions. Admittedly, change and renewal can sometimes be difficult, as "battles" usually are, but this should not detract from the knowledge of the power within us to change.

Paul goes on to explain this battle further in Romans 8:5–7: "For those who live according to the flesh set their minds on the things of the flesh, but those who live according to the Spirit, the things of the Spirit. For to be carnally minded is death, but to be spiritually minded is life and peace. Because the carnal mind is enmity against God; for it is not subject to the law of God, nor indeed can be."

The victory lies in our minds, and where we set, or focus, our minds. If we set our minds on the flesh—worldly perspectives, fears, resentments, jealousies, lusts—the results will bring death or destruction to our lives. Even if we are saved, if our minds are carnal, they are enmity against God, and we will live separated from the strength and blessings of God. As a result, we will not have what it takes to live successfully and to overcome bad habits, negative attitudes, health issues, and relational problems. Our mind-sets actually push us away from our Father in Heaven, and we cannot draw upon His power to move forward in life.

So many of us Christians love the Lord but still struggle in some, or even all, aspects of life because we won't renew our minds to the things of God. We allow our minds to feed on the same newspapers, television programs, and general attitudes that the world does, and so we have the same worldly, carnal mind-set. We live under the authority of the flesh, when biblically speaking, we should be living as people who have been set free from the dominion of the flesh. We should be experiencing life at a higher level in every area.

> So many of us Christians love the Lord but still struggle in some, or even all, aspects of life because we won't renew our minds to the things of God.

If we desire results that produce life, then we must set our minds on the things of the spirit—love, blessing, joy, faith, and God's Word. We need to cultivate a spiritual mind-set if we want to walk in God's perfect will for our lives. What does being "spiritually minded" really mean? Many Christians start to get weird when this topic comes up. They imagine pictures of porky little angels and horned evil demons, and their voices become all sing-song-y and breathy. And then we wonder why the world thinks we're one bubble off center. Having a spiritual mind does not mean you will start seeing ghosts or hearing voices. If this were the case, then I used to be a *very* spiritually minded teenager whenever I smoked enough pot. In addition, it's not walking around thinking about Heaven all the time. If you're too busy picturing the pearly gates and the throne room while you're driving to work, you're going to end up with your bumper wrapped around a tree.

Being spiritually minded and having a renewed mind means, practically speaking, that we possess thoughts that line up with the scriptures. It's choosing to have principles, attitudes, and beliefs that are in agreement with the Word of God. It means whatever you are doing, you do it with a godly perspective. For instance, when you are at work, you work with discipline and integrity; you are the very best because you represent Jesus on the job. When you are interacting with your wife, you treat her as Jesus loves and treats the church. When you are raising your children, you teach them the ways of the Lord; you are leading them as unto the Lord. Instead of operating with a carnal mind, focused only upon your own personal needs and wants, you operate with a spiritual mind, seeking to be unselfish, generous, and loving.

Are you spiritually minded or carnally minded? When stress or temptation arises, do you obey the flesh and respond with anger, gluttony, greed, lust, fear, and depression? Or do you obey the spirit and operate in love, joy, peace, long-suffering, and self-control? Galatians 5:16 teaches, "Walk in the Spirit, and you will not fulfill the lust of the flesh." To be spiritually minded, we need to walk *daily*, plugged into what the Spirit of God is saying to us and how He is leading and guiding us instead of fulfilling the suggestions of the flesh.

It is vital we realize that while our spirits are born again, our flesh never received salvation and it can never be renewed. It will always be drawn to negative addictions and to worldly beliefs, so we must keep it disciplined at all times. Even if we've been walking with God for twenty-five years, we'll never get the luxury of relaxing in the battle of our flesh. It's just like in the training of our kids. We would never say to them, "You guys have been so good about telling the truth all week. You did such a great job not telling any lies. Today for your reward, you can tell all the lies you want. You can do whatever you wish—you deserve it—and tomorrow, we'll get back to telling the truth." This would never happen! Similarly, so must we be consistent with regards to our Christianity and the battle between the spirit and the flesh.

Qualities of the Renewed Mind

1. The renewed mind obeys the Spirit of God and the spirit of the born-again man. Once you have been born again, you have within you more than enough power, wisdom, and perseverance to bring about the change and renewal you desire. The moment you became saved, your human spirit became united with God. According to 1 Corinthians 6:17, "He who is joined to the Lord is one spirit with Him." This is a tremendous revelation if we will meditate on it and press in to understand it.

No matter what your mind-set is today, no matter how entrenched in pain and negativity you might be at this moment, you have dwelling within you the very spirit of the Almighty God. *Nothing* is impossible for you. For you who are already experiencing great successes in your life, you can be assured that because you are united with Him, there remain greater heights and greater victories awaiting you. As Christians, we can live lives that are constantly climbing upward toward more fulfillment, deeper joy, and a closer walk with Jesus Christ. We can know Him more and embrace Him more by renewing our minds.

Too many Christians miss this truth because they are waiting to receive more from God. They aren't attacking their negative mind-sets and the resulting circumstances because they believe they need to receive more of the Holy Spirit before they can engage . . . and so they wait. How can they need *more* of the Holy Spirit? When they were born again, did they only receive an arm and a leg of the Holy Spirit? I've never understood this kind of thinking. You either received Jesus, or you didn't. You were either joined to the Lord and became one spirit with Him, or you weren't.

So many churches get caught up in this "waiting." A couple comes forward for prayer because their marriage is struggling, and the church prays in agreement for a fresh anointing on their marriage and for fresh oil to pour over their relationship. This might feel good momentarily for this couple, but what does this mean for them when they get home? They don't need fresh oil or a fresh anointing. They just need to stop throwing things at each other. They need to decide to not walk in the flesh and start to listen to the Spirit, to obey the Spirit. They need to renew their minds so they can stop being bitter with each other and instead, begin to love each other. You have the fullness of God living on the inside of you—don't wait! You already have everything you need.

2. The renewed mind is aligned with the Word of God.
When we are renewing our minds, we have beliefs that are based upon the Bible, not beliefs derived from the media or from our secular society. We are not swayed by what is popular or politically correct, and when an issue arises about which we are unsure, we go to the Word to find the answers. Consequently, we have a godly perspective about every realm of life. We see through God's eyes of possibility and faith, not through the world's eyes of gloom and doom.

When we have a renewed mind, our attitudes are aligned with God's attitudes. He never sees any of His children as weak and unable. He sees every one of us as champions. Therefore, we don't make excuses for our mistakes or our worldly behavior. We take accountability for our actions and do what is necessary to bring about the positive growth we need. We don't pass the blame on to our culture, our race, or our parents because we see ourselves as children of God, able to overcome every circumstance.

In addition, as we renew our minds, we gain godly imaginations and ways of thinking. We utilize our imaginations to accomplish great things, to see "God ideas" that promote our businesses, to envision prosperous futures, and to propel us forward to help people. We do not desire to imagine the worldly things that are common to many of the people around us like jealousy, paranoia, greed, and lust. We strive not only to find out what the Bible has to say about how and what to think but also to actually put those beliefs into practice by exchanging our thoughts for the thoughts of God.

3. The renewed mind enables us to live in God's will, which is success in life. Our success in life comes as we fulfill God's plan for our lives. When we know that our very lives honor our Father in Heaven, we are filled with a true sense of success in our hearts. We all want to hear God say to us, "Well done!" and when we feel we are on track with His plan, it makes our lives meaningful and productive. There exists no amount of money, sex, or earthly gain that can fulfill us on the inside like the pleasure of our Father, and it is only through a mind that is being renewed to the revelation of His Word that we can discern and accomplish His perfect will for our destinies.

We cannot think like we think today if we want to rise to a higher level in our future. This is going to take new thoughts and new understanding. In Hosea 4:6, God says, "My people are destroyed for lack of knowledge. Because you have rejected knowledge I will also reject you as My priests." He is talking to His own chosen people, not the unbelievers in the world. If the knowledge is available to you and you do not embrace it, then you, just like the children of Israel, are rejecting knowledge. If you have at your fingertips the ability to study God's Word, but you spend all your time with your *People* magazine, *Sports Illustrated*, or with television, movies, and your Wii, then you are rejecting knowledge, and you will not be able to experience a renewed mind or God's perfect will for your life.

Through wisdom a house is built, and by understanding it is established; By knowledge the rooms are filled with all precious and pleasant riches. A wise man is strong, Yes, a man of knowledge increases strength; For by wise counsel you will wage your own war, And in a multitude of counselors there is safety. (Proverbs 24:3–6)

Notice there is nothing in this proverb that suggests we need more of God. We simply need to get our minds aligned with the Word of God, and we will receive an abundant life with great riches. Read this proverb in the New Living Translation: "Any enterprise is built by wise planning, becomes strong through common sense, and profits wonderfully by keeping abreast of the facts. A wise man is mightier than a strong man. Wisdom is mightier than strength. Don't go to war without wise guidance; there is safety in many counselors."

Imagine if you strategized all areas of your life through this revelation. You would find peace, prosperity, and success everywhere you turned. A renewed mind is possible, and every Christian can attain it. Take your time with the next few chapters as they break down how to renew your mind into practical, powerful steps that, if applied, can help you move forward to the quality of life you have always desired.

13 | It Starts in the Soul

At seventeen, the last thing in my life that was prospering was my soul. I felt so empty inside, I tried to find happiness in anything the world could offer: girls, drugs, and cars—especially drugs and cars. Needless to say, combining these two in excessive amounts led to nothing less than disaster, including several handcuffed arrests. Once I met Julius in the drug rehabilitation program, he began to help me understand that everything about my life was conformed to the ways of the world. My mind had gone completely to the carnal and my perspective on life was an unhealthy, self-destructive outlook.

But once I received Jesus and began to learn and to apply new truths, everything in my life began to change. The Word of God became my food, and I didn't view the scriptures merely as good suggestions; I knew they were the keys to my success, and I treated them as such. As I applied the Word in my life—not just believing it or memorizing it but actually putting it into practice in daily life—my soul began to prosper. I met Wendy, we got married, and we began to walk side by side in ministry together. All the while, this cycle of applying God's Word, my soul prospering, and my life getting blessed continued. It was not long before the quality of my life was far beyond anything I ever could have asked or imagined, and that was decades ago! Today, that hurting, drug-addicted teenager is so far behind me, he doesn't even seem part of my past anymore. That old Casey is more like a character in a movie than a real person that once was.

There were many other men and women who were in drug rehab with me during this time. Many who heard the same truths as I did, became Christians like I did, but today haven't found nearly the same success in their lives as I have. Many returned to their drugs and some have died young. Many are struggling through divorces and stuck in unemployment. Why is this? They are Christians, too, so why is their outcome so different than mine? It's not because I'm anything special. It's because even though they heard the Word preached, they never *applied* that truth to their lives. They are saved and will live an eternity with God, but while they are walking on Earth, they will continue to live far below the quality of life God desired for them—unless they begin to renew their minds. It is only then that their souls will begin to prosper, and when that happens, everything around them will begin to flourish as well.

All change, all growth, and all of God's promises are initiated in the realm of the soul: the mind, will, and emotions. When new truth comes into our lives, and we act upon it, our souls will begin to prosper, and as a result, all areas of our lives will start to improve. In our marriages, on our jobs, in our finances, God's prosperity begins to flow through the health of our soul, and we find freedom in those areas that used to hold us back. John 8:31–32 says, "Then Jesus said to those Jews who believed Him, 'If you abide in My word, you are My disciples indeed. And you shall know the truth, and the truth shall make you free.'" If we Christians can grab hold of this truth, embrace this truth, we will possess the ability to go *anywhere* we want in God's will for our lives! When God's truth infiltrates your soul, it begins to prosper, and you are set free from anger, debt, anxiety, fear, and addictions.

Notice Jesus did *not* say you would be a disciple if you regularly attend church or even if you read your Bible every day. There were plenty of Pharisees and other religious rulers during this time who spent hours and hours debating and poring over the scriptures. They were so busy with their religious pursuits they didn't even recognize the Word made flesh, Jesus, standing and teaching right in front of them. They judged Him as a traitor and a false prophet, and they eventually nailed Him to a cross! Jesus said to his followers that if they would abide in His Word, or live in it, breathe it, make it an integral part of their lives, then they could become disciples. Jesus didn't say, "Truth will set you free"; He said *the truth that you know will set you free.* Big difference. Memorizing God's Word does not mean you have any more of a revelation of it than the unbeliever sitting next to you at work. It's only when you seek His Word as your

> When God's truth infiltrates your soul, it begins to prosper, and you are set free from anger, debt, anxiety, fear, and addictions.

very life and begin to obey and to operate by it that you will begin to prosper in your soul and discover the freedom God promises.

Consequently, as our souls prosper, our marriages start to prosper because we are being the right kind of spouses, and our kids grow up to prosper because we brought them up in the knowledge of God's Word. Our finances prosper because we have based our money decisions on the principles of God, and regardless of the world's economy, we consistently have more than enough. Our emotions prosper because we are trusting in God for every area of our lives, and the fear, anxiety, and depression of the world cannot hook us. No matter what comes our way, we can breathe a deep sigh of relief because the truth of God's Word has set us completely free and we can experience total peace.

The "Right" Mind

One of the most famous parables taught by Jesus is the parable of the prodigal son in Luke 15. It's a story of a wealthy man who had two sons, and the younger son asked to receive his inheritance so he could go into the world and enjoy its pleasures. After a short time of drinking, gambling, and evenings spent with prostitutes, he had squandered all of his money and was reduced to working in the fields feeding the hogs. For a Jewish man, this was the epitome of hitting rock bottom, but verse 17 tells us that he finally "came to himself." Other translations say "came to his senses" or "came to his right mind."

It was at this point that he remembered who he was and who his father was. He says, "How many of my father's hired servants have bread enough and to spare, and I perish with hunger! I will arise and go to my father, and will say to him, 'Father, I have sinned against heaven and before you, and I am no longer worthy to be called your son. Make me like one of your hired servants.'" At no time during his years of rebellion did this young man cease from being a son; he was always the son of an upright, wealthy man. But until the day he came to his right mind, he never chose to act like it. Now, he was ready to face the consequences as he humbly sought his father for forgiveness.

How many of us, although we are sons and daughters of the Creator of the Universe, live our lives small, defeated, and scared? We are afraid to go for the dreams we possess in our hearts because we think we'll fail. We are blind to our precious value to our Father so we treat ourselves cheaply, living from boyfriend to boyfriend or offering our bodies to the addictions of drugs and alcohol. We don't believe we can, or in some cases, *should* have abundant finances, so we live from paycheck to paycheck and from credit card statement to credit card statement, never able to be a significant part of establishing God's covenant throughout the earth. We live under the oppression of pain, sickness, and disease because we don't have a revelation of Jesus Christ as our healer. We must be like the prodigal son and come to our right minds, so that we may approach our Father with a willingness to change our mind-sets.

When the prodigal son returned home to his father, the Bible describes a heartfelt reunion. The father, seeing his son at a distance, recognizes him immediately and runs with open arms to embrace his lost son. He loves him, accepts him, and calls for a celebration, complete with the fatted calf and a new robe, ring, and sandals for his son. He says of him in verse 32 that it is right and fitting to celebrate because the young man "was dead and is alive again, was lost and now is found."

What does the father mean when he says his son was dead? He wasn't literally dead; he was out in the world partying and enjoying his sinful behavior. But remember, in the last chapter, we read the scripture from Romans 8:5–6 that says the carnal mind is death and causes exclusion from God while the spiritual mind is life and brings us in union with our Father. The son was dead because he was separated from his father's presence, protection, and provision as a result of his carnal way of thinking and living. He had no access to the wealth and wisdom of his father because he was living his life far apart from him. Once he came to his right mind, he was alive again, and he was able to once again engage in a relationship with his father.

Similarly, many Christians live apart from God, separated from God's supernatural protection and provision because of our carnal ways of thinking and living. We have wrong beliefs, and although we never lose our salvation, or our status as sons and daughters of God, we struggle. Sometimes we go as far as to shake a fist at God, saying, "Why are you doing this to me? Why won't you help me?" That would be like the prodigal son blaming his father for making him end up in the pigsty. How could the father be guilty? He wasn't even there. It was the son's choices that brought him to the pigs, and it was his absence from the ways of his father that brought him to his downfall.

My favorite part of this parable is the father's reaction to the return of his son. Even though the son was thoroughly guilty of much sin, his father greeted him with full acceptance. He didn't say anything that might bring condemnation, and he didn't sentence the son for even one of his "crimes." The father was overjoyed with his arrival, was proud of him for his conversion, and was determined to welcome him and bless him with emotional and physical gifts. This is exactly how our Father in Heaven responds to us when we come to our right minds and seek His forgiveness and His ways. No matter how small or how large our offenses have been, He *never* greets us with condemnation. Romans 8:1 says, "There is therefore no condemnation to those who are in Christ Jesus, who do not walk according to the flesh, but according to the spirit." He is always ready with open arms to embrace each and every one of us with acceptance and blessings. No matter how far or in how many ways we have been living separated from God, let's come to our right minds! Let's seek God's presence and God's ways of thinking, and we will receive a ring, a robe, and a celebration!

The Right Will

When our three children were small, Wendy and I quickly realized we had a trio of very strong-willed kids. As opinionated and driven as both of us are, I really cannot imagine how our kids could have been any other way. As toddlers, it was relatively easy to help them to operate in our wills; if a stern look or voice couldn't do the trick, there was always the spanking spoon to use as a threat. One look at the spoon, and they would quickly submit. But once they became teenagers, it was a whole different scenario. As much as Wendy or I wanted to assert our authority over them when we could see they weren't making the best choices, we had to exercise extreme self-control and let them find out for themselves the consequences of their actions. Now as young adults, it is entirely up to them to choose the ways of God on their own.

Likewise, God cannot force us to engage in His purposes for our lives. We must make a decision on our own to submit our wills to His will. God, knowing the strong sway of the world, gives us some advice. In Deuteronomy 30:19 He says, "I call heaven and earth as witnesses today against you, that I have set before you life and death, blessing and cursing; therefore choose life, that both you and your descendants may live." After giving two options, one resulting in death and one in life, you wouldn't think He would need to instruct us which path to choose! It's almost insulting until we take an honest look at our lives and see how many areas in which we have chosen death. With regard to our spending habits, our eating habits, our recreational habits, and the things we say, so many of us have chosen not to submit our wills to God's will or to submit to what the Bible offers as truth.

> God cannot force us to engage in His purposes for our lives. We must make a decision on our own to submit our wills to His will.

It is up to each Christian to choose to submit his will to the plans and purposes of God. This isn't always easy, and many have a difficult time doing this because their wills have become so weak from atrophy. They have lived so long just following the course of their flesh, or the world, or whatever was expected of them, and now when God proposes a choice, a way to live at a higher level, they cannot seem to make the shift. Your will is like a muscle; it must be exercised in order to become strong to stand against the flow of the flesh and its carnal ways. In some cases, you may simply need to start out by taking small steps toward whatever area in your life you realize you have been operating in the death and cursing option from Deuteronomy 30:19.

One push-up a day isn't very much, but at least it's *something*, and if you add one on each week, in just one year, you'll be doing over fifty push-ups! If you normally eat the entire bag of Cheetos, just eat half the bag, and pretty soon you won't even crave them anymore. Instead of trying to read the entire Bible in a year, just read one scripture a day. Meditate upon that scripture all day, and in one year you will see how much your soul has begun to prosper because of your diligence to apply one of God's principles to your life each day. Every act of positive, biblically based choice strengthens our will and gives us more of an ability to submit our will to God's will.

In Luke 10:38–42, Jesus is visiting two of His good friends, Martha and Mary, and using their house as a place to spend time teaching His disciples. Martha is running around, making sure everyone's needs are met, and trying to fix a meal for all the guests. Then she realizes she doesn't have enough hands to get the job done. When she goes to find her sister, Mary, so she can help, Martha finds her doing no work at all. She's sitting down at the feet of Jesus listening to Him teach. Martha is indignant with the unfairness of this situation. She says to Jesus, "Lord, do You not care that my sister has left me to serve alone? Therefore tell her to help me." Jesus' answer must have surprised her: "Martha, Martha, you are worried and troubled about many things. But one thing is needed, and Mary has chosen that good part, which will not be taken away from her."

While He was not trying to belittle her heart to serve, He wanted her to understand there is a time and a place for everything. It was admirable she was being so diligent, but the higher choice would have been for her to relax and bask in the presence of the Son of God. When it came time for dinner, she could have brought Him whatever she had and said, "Lord, this is all there is; can you bless it and make it enough for everyone?" She could've had both—the satisfaction of offering a wonderful meal to everyone *and* the opportunity to grow in the life-changing power of Jesus' words.

We must get our priorities right. When we put God first, and use our wills to choose to find the time to spend in His Word, we will be able to overcome the debt, the depression, the addictions, and anything that attempts to weigh us down. We will find ourselves living in the blessings and prosperity of God because we decided to submit our wills to God's will for our lives.

Right Emotions

Emotions aren't a curse. Emotions aren't a sign of weakness (are you getting this, guys?), and they aren't uncontrollable (ladies, that's for some of you). We were made in the likeness and image of God, and there are many places in the Bible that depict God showing emotion because of one situation or another. We can find scriptures when He was angry, when He was pleased, when He was disappointed, and when He was jealous. Jesus, as the Son of God, was the perfect example of being a man fully in touch with His emotions, but never letting them get out of control. We read about His anger with the moneychangers in the temple, His surprise at the lack (and the abundance) of certain people's faith, His grief at the tomb of Lazarus, and His compassion as He healed the masses. By His sinless model, it's clear that it's never wrong to feel emotions about any situation; it's simply a matter of how we respond to them.

Sometimes our Christian teaching can lead us to believe that it is acceptable to feel positive emotions like happiness and pleasure, but unacceptable to express negative ones like anger and frustration. Ephesians 4:26–27 sheds some light on the issue for us. It says, "'Be angry, and do not sin': do not let the sun go down on your wrath, nor give place to the devil." Paul doesn't tell us not to be angry; in fact, he says that it is fine to be angry—just don't sin because of it, or let it linger longer than a few hours, or else you will give the enemy a foothold in your life.

Feeling emotions will not keep us out of God's perfect will for our lives. Attempting to hide or suppress every negative emotion will only lead to a physical or mental breakdown of some degree. Eventually, these stresses will spring up as cancer, depression, sickness, or panic attacks. We must allow ourselves to feel the emotions that rise up inside of us, but then choose to line them up with godly thoughts and godly actions. Be angry, but don't punch a hole in the wall. Get yourself together before you react, and then respond in a right way. Feel the fear, but don't let it take hold in your heart or become any part of your speech. Find scriptures that offer God's promises for that situation and speak His life-giving Word over it until faith begins to arise. Recognize the laziness, and then do something about it. Get up off the couch and do a jumping jack or something! Paul gives a powerful guide to handling our emotions.

1. Feel the emotion.

2. Resist the temptation to sin because of that emotion.

3. Resolve that negative emotion in some way before you go to bed.

The soul is where the abundance and blessing of God resides, and every Christian has one. When we get our minds, wills, and emotions right, we will begin to experience the exciting life of renewal God has planned for us. Each day, we will become stronger as we align our lives with His Word, and the weaknesses that used to bring us frustration and failure will start to fade away. When we have God's prosperity flowing from our souls, we will have everything we need within us to empower us for higher heights in every realm of our destinies.

14 | The Focus of Renewal

A man came up to me after a church service and said, "I tried your renewing the mind deal, and it really worked. Thanks!" As he walked away, I thought, *That guy just doesn't get it.* Renewing the mind isn't something you "did." It's something you are doing every day, something you are committed to never stop going for—it's a lifestyle.

In the Greek language, there is a unique verb tense. Like English, Greek has past, present, and future verb tenses, but it also has one that means the action is continual; it never ends or is something we are always engaged in. In Romans 12:2, when Paul wrote, "Be transformed by the renewing of your mind," he used that ongoing verb tense with the word *transformed*. He was trying to get us to understand that this renewal was a process, a constant challenge for every Christian to grab hold of throughout their entire lives. When we understand this and choose to be a part of this daily discipline, we will be able to experience God's perfect will for our lives.

We know this idea of ongoing growth is true for our kids. If they do not like a particular season of their lives, we say, "Don't worry, son. Not long from now you'll have grown out of this awkward stage." Or "You're so young right now; I promise you'll understand this when you're older." We encourage them to move forward in their lives by explaining that positive rewards will come if they will only continue to learn new things and keep their visions fresh. We tell them they can do anything, change anything, if they will make sure to not let their frustrations keep them down. When did we stop believing this to be true for *ourselves* and give up on the attitude to be ever ready to grow, to change, and to renew? When did we start putting our minds on hold and settle for living every day by a predictable set of habits and routines? Some of us have put our brains on birth control; we haven't given birth to a new thought in years!

None of us are living our lives exactly how we want them. While there are many aspects we love, we all have areas and habits we are dissatisfied with. But the Bible tells us that we can change whatever realms of life we aren't happy with, if we will only choose to embrace this idea of change and renewal. Instead of thinking this year will be the "same old, same old," we can look forward to the next year being the best one yet, no matter how old we are. Rather than making excuses about why we can never change, we can opt to make choices to think differently, to act differently, and to experience life differently.

New Skin, New Thoughts

The book of James was written by one of the natural brothers of Jesus. If anyone needed to renew his mind, it was James. How would you like to wake up one day and realize your older brother is God? Not only have you spent your life getting his hand-me-down tunics, trying to live up to the brother that never did anything wrong, but now you are faced with the fact He is God! How do you compete with *that*? It must have been tough for James to rethink the image he had of his brother, but he did eventually become a Christian and a pastor of a thriving church. James gives us great insight into the process of renewing the mind: "Therefore lay aside all filthiness and overflow of wickedness, and receive with meekness the implanted word, which is able to save your souls" (James 1:21).

I love the King James Version of this scripture: "Wherefore lay apart all filthiness and superfluity of naughtiness, and receive with meekness the engrafted word, which is able to save your souls." Superfluity of naughtiness—that just rolls off the tongue, doesn't it?

James says it is the *engrafted* word that possesses the power to save our souls. Not the word that we heard, the word that we read, or the word that we memorized. Saying "Amen!" in church but then forgetting the sermon before we leave the parking lot won't do much to save our souls. This is why many folks can go to church for years and never change their lives for the better. Remember, all prosperity flows out of our souls, and the mind (which is the prominent part of the soul) is where true renewal starts. James teaches us we must be diligent to make sure God's Word is engrafted into our souls, not just lying on top of them.

All prosperity flows out of our souls, and the mind (which is the prominent part of the soul) is where true renewal starts.

We have a young man in our church who served in Iraq during the first year of the second Iraq war. He was involved in a massive explosion and miraculously lived to tell the story. However, he suffered extensive wounds on his back, which required skin grafts because the injuries to his skin were too wide and too deep to heal on their own. The doctors harvested a piece of skin from one part of his body so they could perform a skin graft procedure. They used the new skin to cover the wound on his back, and eventually that graft attached itself and began to operate as if it had always been there. The recovery process took a few months, but today the skin is completely healed, so well in fact, you can hardly see any scars and would never know he had received a skin graft.

When we engraft the Word of God into our lives, it has a similar effect. We hear the Word, and then we accept it, believe it, confess it, and begin to live it. James teaches us in verses 22–25 this engrafting of the Word is a progression:

> But be doers of the word, and not hearers only, deceiving yourselves. For if anyone is a hearer of the word and not a doer, he is like a man observing his natural face in a mirror; for he observes himself, goes away, and immediately forgets what kind of man he was. But he who looks into the perfect law of liberty and

continues in it, and is not a forgetful hearer but a doer of the
work, this one will be blessed in what he does.

When we implant the Word in our hearts and actually apply
it in our lives by thinking and acting differently, then our soul is
affected and our lives begin to change. The blessings of God,
which were once hindered by a wounded soul, can now begin to
flow out through the health spreading inside our souls. Again,
the results don't happen overnight, but if we will be consistent,
the renewal is inevitable. Renewal will become such a normal
part of our lives, we cannot imagine settling for anything
less than God's best. Our old beliefs and old habits will dissolve
away and God's new and higher ways will reign in our everyday
lives.

Once, you used to stomp around and yell at your family, but
because you have been engrafting in your heart God's Word
about gentleness and self-control, you are able to respond in a
peaceful way. Before, your life was always one financial crisis followed by another, but now because you have begun to think
God's thoughts about finances, you see something different.
You begin to make Bible-based choices in the area of money, you
gain an understanding about the godly principles regarding
money, and your finances start to climb upward. Or you used to
be afraid all the time, scared for your kids, scared about current events, scared about your health, but then the engrafted
Word begins to produce God's peace that passes understanding,
and now you are able to ditch the tranquilizers and sleep at
night.

Don't Look at the Rock

In my twenties and thirties, I was an avid bicycle racer. Even in Seattle with its many months of rain, I would train almost every day for the next race. Miles and miles, through rough terrain and steep hills, I would ride with a few of my cycling friends. Once, a buddy and I completed the Seattle to Portland annual race, riding about two hundred miles in just ten hours. It is an exciting, healthy, and time-consuming sport.

One of the major disciplines for every cyclist is focus. Whether racing around corners just inches away from the other bikes in the pack or speeding down mountains in a bicycle lane barely ten inches wide, it was imperative to keep my eyes focused upon where I wanted to go next. If I was worried about colliding with the bike next to me, and I fixed my eyes on its wheels instead of the road ahead, chances are I would accidentally steer my bike toward that wheel and clip the other rider's bike. The very thing I was trying to prevent would happen, and before I knew it, a chain reaction of crashes would cause many of us to become tangled in a mess of wrecked bicycles. No matter what was going on around me—bad weather, crashes around me, or other distractions—I would be able to avoid skidding across the surface of the road if I simply stayed disciplined to look straight ahead.

Whatever it is that we are spending most of our time focusing on is the very thing we will cause to happen in our lives.

This concept is *key* to renewing the mind and engrafting God's thoughts into our lives.

Whatever it is that we are spending most of our time focusing on is the very thing we will cause to happen in our lives. Just like the cyclist, if we have our eyes fixed on the rocks in the road, the things we *don't* want to have in our lives, even though we want to avoid them, we will steer our lives straight toward them. It's not a matter of what you *desire* for your life; it's a matter of what you decide to fix your eyes upon. In Colossians 3:1–2, Paul writes, "If then you were raised with Christ, seek those things which are above, where Christ is, sitting at the right hand of God. Set your mind on things above, not on things on the earth".

We must set our minds on the ways and the principles of God. Again, this does not mean focusing up at the sky trying to see a glory cloud descending from Heaven. It means whatever you are doing throughout the day, you do it with a godly perspective. And it takes effort to set your mind on things above because everything around us in the world is trying to grab our attention. With the world's advertisements everywhere we look, and its attitudes in many of the people around us, we have to make a choice to think in a different way. Unless we purposefully steer our minds toward the paths we want our lives to follow, we will automatically find ourselves along the ways of the world and its carnal lifestyle.

To set our minds means to exercise our minds, to stretch our brains. When was the last time you exercised your brain and thought in a new way? If we were able to take a picture of the health of your mind, what would it look like—a big blob lounging in an easy chair or a strong, fit, and active force? The way to make your brain and mind strong and active is by taking an interest in furthering your obedience to God. Most seem to have time to watch TV and many read all of the celebrity gossip, but how much time do we spend involved with God's Word? Whenever I hear someone say they don't have time to read the Bible or pray and have fellowship with God, I want to shout, "Liar! You are totally lying to me right now!" Of course, my tender and compassionate pastoral heart overpowers these urges and I keep myself under control. But the truth is we all have the time. We choose not to spend the time focused on the ways of God because we are more interested in other things.

However, if we want to move forward in our lives, we need to get ourselves focused on the things of God. We must set our minds on His thoughts and His ways. When we stretch our minds and exercise our brains, we are engaged in this continual process of renewal, and we are able to stay young. If we'll learn something new and choose to think new thoughts, we'll stay pliable and ready to go for greater dreams and goals. Growing old is simply a matter of mind-set, and this can happen when we are twenty-five or when we are ninety-five. There are some ninety-five-year-olds walking around as if they were younger than a twenty-five-year-old who has stopped embracing new challenges and new ways of thinking. Let's decide to stay young and purposefully set our minds on things above, not on the things of this earth.

Have you ever had an opportunity to do something new come your way and you thought, *I'm not going to be afraid. I'm not going to be afraid. I'm not going to allow myself to be afraid this time and mess things up. I'm not going to focus on the fear or the sweaty hands or the heart palpitations. I'm going to go in there, and*

I will not be afraid... What happened? You were afraid! You spent so much time psyching yourself out trying *not* to be afraid, the fear was all you could think about! You can't not think about it by thinking about not thinking about it. (Did you get that? You might need to read that last sentence again.)

We can't get rid of fear (or any other type of negative habit) by focusing on it. If all we are thinking about is the fear, then that's all we are going to experience. If we want something different, then we need to set our minds on something different; we need to feed our courage and starve the fear. Instead of negative thoughts, we can choose to think God's thoughts: "God has not given me a spirit of fear, but one of power, love and a sound mind" (2 Timothy 1:7). "Greater is He that is in me than he that is in the world" (2 John 4:4). "[A]nd the peace of God, which surpasses all understanding, will guard your hearts and minds through Christ Jesus" (Philippians 4:7). If we will discipline ourselves to meditate on these thoughts and exercise our minds to focus on courage instead of fear, all of a sudden we will begin to feel strong on the inside and our fears will fade away.

This is an example of setting our minds on things above. It means we focus on what we want, instead of what we don't want. This seems almost too simple, doesn't it? It may not be rocket science, but it will change your life if you will embrace it! Any area of our lives that is negative or is below the level we want it to be, we can change it. If we will spend the time to engraft God's Word into our lives by aligning our thoughts to His thoughts, we will be able to discover the renewal and the victory we have been searching for.

The Race Toward Renewal

In a fast, challenging race, runners are trained to never look behind them. Even a glance back at their competition can take hundredths of a second off their time, and that split second can be the difference between a first-place win and a second-place finish. The sprinters are not looking at the other competitors or at the spectators in the stands; they are looking forward to the prize ahead of them. In our walk with Jesus, we must cultivate this same type of forward vision. In Philippians 3:12b–14, Paul teaches, "I press on, that I may lay hold of that for which Christ Jesus has also laid hold of me. Brethren, I do not count myself to have apprehended; but one thing I do, forgetting those things which are behind and reaching forward to those things which are ahead, I press toward the goal for the prize of the upward call of God in Christ Jesus."

Just like the fear example in the previous section, if we allow ourselves to focus our thoughts on anything except the positive results we are aiming for, we will never find ourselves capturing the prize of the upward call of God. Notice Paul writes God's will for our lives is an "upward" call. Every day, every month, every year, it is God's desire that we continually experience more and more of His blessings and abundance in our lives. If we lock our minds on His promises, we will see this come to pass, but if we hesitate to press forward, and keep looking behind into the pain and disappointments of our past, we will never be able to walk in His destiny and His perfect will for our lives.

So many of us have been hurt by someone or by something in

our past: abuse, abandonment, rejection, and even our own poor choices have left painful scars in our souls. As a result, we are stuck in anger and bitterness, unable to forgive, and we can't move forward or reach for the next level of life. Only the power of God's Word can rescue us from the hold of our past. Remember, James said it was the engrafted Word that has the power to save our souls. This includes any pain we might harbor from our past. God's Word is big enough and powerful enough to bring healing to our hearts—*if* we will allow it. This process of healing may not be easy and may take some time, but God's Word *will* set us free from our pasts if we will press forward and receive His restoration.

Philippians 4:8 says, "Finally, brethren, whatever things are true, whatever things are noble, whatever things are just, whatever things are pure, whatever things are lovely, whatever things are of good report, if there is any virtue and if there is anything praiseworthy—meditate on these things." Just like setting our minds on the things we desire, "forgetting those things which are behind" takes an attitude and a discipline to engage in God's Word, to think on God's Word. We must focus on the promises of God, not just for our futures, but also for our day-to-day lives. Proverbs 23:7 tells us that "as a man thinks in his heart, so is he." We have the power within us to be healthy and whole in our hearts or to be weak and victimized. We cannot change our pasts, but we can change how we *think* about our pasts. We cannot change the abuse, but we can choose to forgive and to receive God's healing. We cannot change the poor choices we made, but we can learn from our mistakes and choose to grow in God's Word. We can choose to meditate on His Word.

15 The Spirit of the Mind

Many Christians live their entire lives never understanding how they can change those areas with which they have struggled, and even though they had a sincere desire to be different, they never initiated the process of renewal. Desire to change, no matter how strong it may be, will never be enough to experience lasting change in our lives. In order to be different, to live life at a higher level, we need new revelation and deeper understanding of the principles of God. This goes beyond just hearing weekly sermons and believing the Bible. This renewal takes a diligence to move beyond the surface of our lives. It requires an honest look within the core of who we are, the inner man, the subconscious ... the spirit of the mind.

Have you ever been around someone, and even though he said nice things and acted in the right way, you just didn't get a good feeling about him? You might say that he "gives off the wrong vibe" or that "there's something about him I can't seem to put my finger on, but it's just not right." Any way you phrase it, what you are trying to say is that there is something we cannot see, something coming from the core of who he is that isn't right. Maybe he's hurting in his heart, has major insecurities, or even has wrong motives, and no matter what he says or does, the feeling he gives off makes others feel uncomfortable. We are referring to the spirit of the man, or the spirit of his mind.

Another way to explain it is this: Have you ever told a friend you didn't like something (a food, a type of television show, or a style of clothing) and when that friend asked you why, you just said, "I don't know, I just don't like it"? Later, when you thought about it, you realized you didn't have any reason why you had the opinion you did. You don't know why you didn't like it, you just didn't. Again, it has to do with the spirit of your mind, or your subconscious. If you thought long enough, you probably could find what the true reasons were behind your preference. Maybe your mom didn't like that thing, or a person who once hurt you did like it and that thing reminds you of that situation. Whatever the case may be, every one of us has beliefs and preferences that are rooted in our subconscious minds, or the spirit of our minds, and through the course of our lives we simply go along with these beliefs without recognizing them or asking what truths they are based upon.

Ephesians 4:22–24 gives us some insight. Paul says to "put off, concerning your former conduct, the old man which grows corrupt according to the deceitful lusts, *and be renewed in the spirit of your mind,* and that you put on the new man which was created according to God, in true righteousness and holiness" (emphasis added). Here Paul makes a unique distinction. In other writings he writes about being transformed by the renewing of our minds, and here he talks about being renewed in the *spirit* of our minds. This renewal goes to the core of each person, to the inner being, and enables us to change those thoughts, habits, and addictions embedded deep within the subconscious. Renewing the mind allows us to change the way we think; renewing the spirit of our mind allows us to change why we think the way we think.

Dr. David Yonggi Cho, who is the founder and senior pastor of the largest church in the world, Yoido Full Gospel Church in Seoul, Korea, was visiting our church, Christian Faith Center. After he taught one of our services, he invited Wendy and me to lunch.

> Renewing the mind allows us to change the way we think; renewing the spirit of our mind allows us to change why we think the way we think.

He had been out of his country for some time and was craving a good home-cooked Korean meal. We have many people in our congregation who were born in Korea, so several of the ladies fixed Dr. Cho a huge spread of authentic Korean cuisine and delivered it to his hotel room. When we arrived, there were tables of various delicacies: squid, octopus, kimchi, and some other things I had never seen before.

Dr. Cho was thrilled as he ate everything, commenting on how wonderful it all tasted. Meanwhile, Wendy and I would smile and take small bites, and say, "Yum." Then after we left, we drove somewhere to get some "real" food. Every bit of that

Korean food tasted delicious to Dr. Cho. It reminded him of the food he grew up on, the smells of his home country, and he savored each dish. Why did he love it so much while all Wendy and I could think was, *Do you have any ketchup to put on this? Where's the A-1 sauce?* It's all in the subconscious.

Cultures have their own ways, habits, and foods, and whatever culture you grew up in, in general you will automatically like the things that spring from your heritage. These beliefs become part of your subconscious and the spirit of your mind. Each culture differs from another, has its own ways and attitudes, and usually looks upon another culture's ways as different and often strange. Just like Dr. Cho loved the squid and couldn't imagine anyone thinking otherwise, Wendy and I looked at that very same squid and couldn't imagine why anyone would put it in his mouth *on purpose*. We were raised in different cultures and, likewise, developed different preferences and beliefs.

Many of the reactions, attitudes, and feelings we have toward things are not conscious choices. We like things simply because we do, and that's that. Why we favor certain foods, why we are attracted to certain types of people, why we struggle with particular emotions or weaknesses—most of this has to do with our subconscious minds. Whole cultures generate opinions on issues or have certain prejudices and beliefs without analyzing them or thinking through them as they are passed from generation to generation. Both positive habits and negative habits; every one of us has ways of thinking we "inherited" from our parents and grandparents, and unless we stop to think about why we are how we are, we can never change.

It doesn't really matter why we believe what we believe or

why we like what we like. In fact, we can spend hundreds of hours with therapists and self-help books and maybe we could discover the answers to "why," but at the end of the day, knowing the "why" behind the "what" isn't going to help us live a better life. The only question we need to ask ourselves is, do my beliefs, attitudes, and feelings align with the Word of God? In the areas where the answer is "yes," we can be encouraged. In the areas where the answer is "no," we can see a great opportunity for renewal!

Don't Be a Knee Jerk

If you are alive, you have physical reflexes, and when you visit the doctor, he takes a little hammer and taps your knee to test them. As soon as that hammer makes contact with your knee, your leg kicks. You don't have to tell your leg to kick; it moves on its own as a response to the hammer. In fact, even if you try not to kick, your leg will still fly up automatically when the doctor taps you. It's a reflex action, or an involuntary movement caused by a certain stimulus, and we have many types of these reflexes in our bodies. As you are reading this book right now, your body is digesting food and your heart is beating, even though you haven't been thinking about these organs or telling them to work. They just work because of reflex actions and not because of any conscious decisions on your part. The same thing happens in our thought life.

We all have reflexive thoughts and reactions; many people call them "knee-jerk" reactions. A situation happens or someone says something, and you get mad. Your face gets flushed, your blood pressure rises, your stomach starts to churn, and you are angry. You didn't stop and think to yourself, "I'm going to get mad right now. I think I'm about ready to have a fit." You simply got mad; it was a knee-jerk reaction. You're not quite sure why you became so angry; you can't explain it, but the thing just set you off. The person next to you experienced the same circumstance, and they didn't get mad. In fact, they're saying, "Why are you so upset about this? You are overreacting because it's not that big of a deal." Now, you're mad at them for not being mad with you *and* for judging you for your obvious lack of self-control.

The issue isn't what happened; it's the spirit of your mind. We have subconscious thoughts that lie underneath the surface of our habits, emotions, and attitudes, and these thoughts trigger responses when they are "tapped" by the hammers of our day-to-day experiences. Whether it's fear, anger, jealousy, lust, whatever, we all have operated in this type of knee-jerk reaction. Without a thought, we respond to a situation by feeling rejected, feeling judged, or feeling intimidated, and later when we take a moment to figure out why we feel the way we do, we can't explain it. It's the spirit of our minds.

I'm convinced most of the conflicts we face with our spouses and friends stem from subconscious thoughts and attitudes we don't even know we have. During the early years of ministry when I used to counsel married couples, I met a couple on the brink of divorce because they were so upset about which way the toilet paper fed and how the toothpaste tube was squeezed. Another couple, separated over a disagreement over the wife cutting her hair, came in. The husband was furious with her and could not believe she would do such a terrible thing. I remember thinking, *Really? Hair? You're in a crisis because of hair? You should be happy to have a wife!* He could not explain why he felt so betrayed, but he knew he didn't like it and was convinced it was wrong. He was ready to throw in the towel of his marriage because of a trip to the salon. Knee-jerk reactions.

Most of the thoughts and beliefs within our subconscious were formed by the modeling of our parents. While culture and environment play an important role, usually these factors are consistent with what decisions our guardians made and how they responded to life events. For some of us this is a great truth, but for others it's downright scary. Some of us look at our parents and promise ourselves we will never end up like they have, but unless we go to work at renewing the spirit of our minds, our future will not be much different than theirs.

Was That My Dad?

When my first son, Caleb, was born, I was very excited to give him his first bath. Wendy was resting from the labor and delivery, and I got the privilege to wash him and dress him in his first outfit. A few friends were there with a camcorder recording the event as I played and talked to Caleb and scrubbed him clean. Days later, when Wendy and I watched the video, I was shocked to see myself looking and sounding just like my father. I acted toward Caleb like my dad had acted toward me, and I recognized my father's spirit and his attitude coming out of me as I related to my child. It freaked me out! By now I had spent more than a decade aggressively working to renew the spirit of my mind and to be very *unlike* my father. If this was seeping from me when Caleb was just an hour old, what was going to happen when he was twelve or sixteen? At that moment, I realized I had to get serious about renewing the spirit of my mind because I knew how I ended up under my dad's training, and I certainly didn't want my kids to find themselves in the same place.

Most of what has been programmed into our minds came from our parents. As we matured, we just picked up all of their thoughts and attitudes. Of course, most parents do not purposely set out to plant negative habits into the lives of their children, but modeling is the most powerful influence in a person's life. Good or bad, what our parents did and how they acted was what we saw every day of our lives, and we sucked up like a sponge everything that spilled out of them. Now, unless we stop to analyze ourselves, we will move through our lives responding and acting very similarly to them, unless we engage in God's process of renewal.

Hebrews 12:14–15 gives us great insight about the dynamics behind renewing the spirit of our minds: "Pursue peace with all people, and holiness, without which no one will see the Lord: looking carefully lest anyone fall short of the grace of God; lest any

> The commitment to renewing the spirit of our minds must be sincere and it must be persistent. If we want to rise above what was modeled in our lives and get beyond a shallow Christianity, we must have a heartfelt, deep desire to take steps daily to renew the spirit of our minds.

root of bitterness springing up cause trouble, and by this many become defiled." We must pursue peace, holiness, and all the things of God; we must be always looking carefully so that we can maintain a consistent walk with God. Otherwise, it says a root of bitterness could spring up and cause us to stumble. Let's explore this further.

First, *pursue* is a key word here. The commitment to renewing the spirit of our minds must be sincere and it must be persistent. If we want to rise above what was modeled in our lives and get beyond a shallow Christianity, we must have a heartfelt, deep desire to take steps daily to renew the spirit of our minds. It's one thing to consciously get new information and have a conscious understanding in your mind of what you are trying to accomplish; it's a whole other thing to try to change the *spirit* of our minds, to change our subconscious thinking, to reprogram our "autopilot." We cannot achieve this renewal if we are once-a-month Christians or once-a-week Bible scholars. It's going to take much more than our weekly church services and our random prayer and study times. We need to decide to be daily Christians. What we do monthly or weekly might bring temporary change to our lives, but what we do daily will bring the change and renewal we truly are longing for. It's what we choose *daily* that will make an impact on the spirit of our minds.

Second, the writer of Hebrews uses the phrase "root of bitterness." A root is below the surface, something you cannot see. Have you ever had weeds growing in your yard or garden that you tried over and over to get rid of? It's not good enough to simply cut the weed down or break it off at its stem. If you don't pull the weed up from its roots, that thing will grow right back no matter how many times you attempt to kill it. Its root system can run very deep in the soil and sometimes can be much bigger than the actual weed above ground. As long as the root remains, there will always be a weed ready to spring up.

So it goes with our beliefs and our thought life. Our spirit of the mind is below the surface. It's the root system that feeds our actions and feelings. And if we are not carefully staying alert, just as the passage says, a root can spring up and cause trouble in our lives: roots of bitterness, roots of fear, roots of anger, and roots of depression, anxiety, lust, or any other negative feeling. These roots spring up and cause us to do things we are ashamed of and wish we hadn't done. They act as anchors in our lives and disable us from breaking free from the food, the sex, the drugs, the low self-esteem, the world. We must make a decision to deal with these roots because otherwise they will control our lives and keep us from the life we really want with God.

But here's the good news. If you have a negative root system, you can decide to change it and grow a positive root system. If you pursue God's renewal, you can exchange a negative spirit of the mind for one that is full of faith and confidence! As a Christian, you have the power within you to achieve the amazing destiny God designed for you, but it's going to take a spirit of the mind that is aligned to God's ways and God's Word. You can break that addiction, you can lose that weight, you can overcome that fear and that depression, but you cannot do it with the same spirit of the mind you are working with right now. It's going to take new habits of thinking, a new revelation of God's Word, and a renewal of the spirit of your mind.

16 | Get the Egypt Out!

I n my early twenties, after I had gone through Washington Drug Rehabilitation Program, I spent hundreds of hours giving back to the program through counseling. I'll never forget one guy I was helping—or at least I thought I was helping. This young man was a heroin addict in a major life crisis involving all sorts of drugs and the crimes that went with them. His life was going from hell to hell. As Christians, we are supposed to be living lives going from glory to glory, but for those entangled in the world, their lives just go from hell to hell.

We had spent many hours together, and on this particular day, I believed I was finally getting through to him. I was saying, "Bro, you can whoop this addiction and this behavior. God's got a plan for your life, and if you would just change who you are, you could have a great life!" At that moment, he suddenly sat up, and I saw the lights had gone on behind his eyes. Taking his alertness as agreement, I went on, "Trust me, I understand it'll be difficult at first, but we'll all help you make the changes you need to make. We'll get you new friends, help you create new habits, and most of all, help you think and act differently."

"Wait a minute," he said. "Am I hearing you right? You want *me* to be a different person?"

"Yes! That's exactly it! If you'll just change who you are, you will be able to overcome all this junk and get on with a great life."

He gave me a strange look and said, "Well, I know I need to stop the drugs, and I know I need to stop the crime, but as far as I'm concerned, I'm not that bad of a person. And neither are my friends, for that matter. I don't need to be a different person. I'm outta here!" And the guy stood up and left. Two months later, he was dead. He wanted to lose the drugs, the crime, and the parole officer, but he didn't want to renew the spirit of his mind, so instead of opting for the life God had for him, he chose to stay in the world, and he died in his addiction.

This experience impacted me, and I think about that guy every now and then when I hear Christians complaining to God about their negative circumstances. So many Christians want to live at a higher level, but they are waiting on the circumstances to be different before they engage in a deeper pursuit of God. The Bible says you and I need to be transformed by the renewing of our minds and *then* the situations will change. If we wait for the pounds to fall off or the money to roll in, if we wait for the fear to go away before we decide to grab hold of the renewal God has for us, nothing in our lives will ever get better. If we can get past the shallow, conscious level of our lives and make some deep, heartfelt changes that affect the spirit of our minds, *then* the other things will change also.

It may sound simple, but renewing the spirit of our minds is hard to do. It is so much easier to think like the world because everyone around you agrees with you. When you listen to the radio, turn on the television, and read the news, nothing you see and hear will ever confront or challenge you because you all think the same way. To float downstream with secular society takes much less effort than attempting to swim upstream against the current, but we are trying to think differently because we are trying to think biblically. Any ol' dead fish can float downstream, but it takes faith, fight, purpose, and desire to battle the current and swim upstream. Are you a dead fish or a strong, fast king salmon?

Caleb Had a Different Spirit

In Numbers, we find the children of Israel ready to approach their Promised Land. God had just miraculously delivered them out from under their slavery which had lasted for generations in Egypt. These people had witnessed some of the most incredible signs and wonders recorded in the Old Testament, and now all they needed to do was cross the Jordan River and enter into Canaan, the land of abundance God had promised to them. Chapter 13 records the people picking twelve spies to go and investigate the land so they would know the best way to take over and possess Canaan.

The spies went to survey the land, and when they came back,

with the exception of two, Caleb and Joshua, they gave a bad report to the children of Israel. They said the people in that land were too strong to be defeated. The crowds of Jews began to talk all at once, but it says in verse 30, "Then Caleb quieted the people before Moses, and said, 'Let us go up at once and take possession, for we are well able to overcome it.' But the men who had gone up with him said, 'We are not able to go up against the people, for they are stronger than we... There we saw the giants; and we were like grasshoppers in our own sight, and so we were in their sight.'"

The account goes on to tell how the entire congregation not only fell to their faces and wept but also began to wish they could go back to the safety of their old lives of slavery in Egypt! How is it possible that these people, who had just defeated the most advanced and powerful army in the world, could be crying like babies over a group of men who were not half as strong as the Egyptian army? They had witnessed incredible manifestations of God's power and now were doubting He would come through for them. Rather than trust in the promises God gave them, they chose to believe their doubts and wish they were back in slavery!

God had gotten the children of Israel out of Egypt, but He was not able to get Egypt out of them; He had delivered them from slavery, but He could not get the slavery out of them. Even though they were a free people, they still saw themselves as slaves, as weak, and as poor. God Himself could not make them see themselves differently, and their mind-sets of poverty and the negative spirit of their minds kept them from going into their promised land. As a result, God said, "Because all these men who have seen My glory and the signs which I did in Egypt and in the wilderness, and have put Me to the test now these ten times, and have not heeded My voice, they certainly shall not see the land of which I swore to their fathers, nor shall any of those who rejected Me see it" (Numbers 14:22–23).

But Caleb was set apart from these people. In verse 24, God says, "But My servant Caleb, because he has a different spirit in him and has followed Me fully, I will bring into the land where he went, and his descendants shall inherit it." What did God mean when He said Caleb had a different spirit? None of these people had the Holy Spirit—that wouldn't be available until Jesus came, died on the cross, and sent His Holy Spirit. Caleb was human and, under the old covenant, just like the others. How could he have a different spirit?

God was referring to Caleb's spirit of his mind. He didn't think like the rest of them, and he didn't allow himself to have that old negative, poverty-stricken slave mentality. While the other spies were yelling, "We be not able!" Caleb was shouting, "Let's go up *at once* and possess the land!" He believed in the prophet Moses, he trusted in the promises of God, and he thought that if God had gotten them out of Egypt, then He would easily help them defeat these giants. While the other spies were confessing their miseries, Caleb was trying to inspire them, "We'll have our own farms, and our own cities!" But he was the only one, and his voice was drowned out by the other ones.

So many of us are like the children of Israel. We've accomplished the most amazing things, overcome some of the most tragic circumstances, and here we are with nothing but potential and opportunity ahead of us. We've gotten ourselves educated, found a wonderful spouse, and are enjoying a good life serving God. We've killed some giants in our day! Then, all of a sudden, we hit a point when a challenge seems too big. We get nervous, start doubting ourselves and think, *I can't do this. It'll never work. I just can't go any further.* So we start to back up and we get stuck. The spirit of our minds starts to take over and we become grasshoppers in our own sight. Let's choose instead to have a Caleb spirit, to renew the spirit of our minds and think, *Good thing those giants are so big—now I'll never miss them!* Let's eat giants for breakfast! And the rewards of having a Caleb spirit are so worth it.

While every Jew who had doubted the Word of God was sentenced to a life of wandering through and dying in the desert, never getting to see the Promised Land, Caleb had a much different fate. After forty-five years of waiting, Caleb and Joshua led the children of Israel on to victory into the land of Canaan. When it came time for dividing the inheritance of the land among the people, Caleb said in Joshua 14:7–12:

I was forty years old when Moses the servant of the Lord sent me from Kadesh Barnea to spy out the land, and I brought back word to him as it was in my heart. Nevertheless my brethren who went up with me made the heart of the people melt, but I wholly followed the Lord my God. So Moses swore on that day, saying, "Surely the land where your foot has trodden shall be your inheritance and your children's forever, because you have wholly followed the Lord my God."

And now, behold, the Lord has kept me alive, as He said, these forty-five years, ever since the Lord spoke this word to

Moses while Israel wandered in the wilderness; and now, here I
am this day, eighty-five years old. As yet I am as strong this day
as on the day that Moses sent me; just as my strength was then,
so now is my strength for war, both for going out and for coming
in. Now therefore, give me this mountain of which the Lord spoke
in that day.

Let's be like Caleb—ready to stand in faith for as long as it
takes and to believe in the promises of God no matter what
everyone around us is saying. Let's have a different spirit of the
mind than the world has. When the modern-day prophets of
doom speak, let's be the ones to oppose them and say, "Let's go
up at once and possess it!" When everyone else is cutting back,
we know God is going to allow us to prosper anyway because we
don't flow with the world economy; we operate in the economy
of Heaven. When the people around us are scared of the wars,
the rumors of war, and the uncertainty of the times, we do not
waver in fear, but walk by faith in God's perfect peace. Let's not
allow ourselves to float downstream in the negativity of the
world. Let's follow God, trust in God, obey God, and see what
God can do in our lives!

The Five *D*s

Renewing the spirit of our minds takes a deeper level of desire
and commitment to change than the average person possesses.
But you and I are not average. We are filled with the life of God
and the power of the Holy Spirit, and we are like Caleb; we are set

apart from the world. We don't settle for mediocrity, and we are going for God's best! There are five keys, five *D*s, that will help us stay focused on this journey of renewal and change:

1. Desire. We must desire to experience a higher level of living, a deeper walk with God. Just feeling like we "should" will never produce long-term results. That "should" feeling is always accompanied by guilt and condemnation, and these two forces cannot produce motivation. They just make us feel bad about ourselves and think we are not good enough to go the distance. We must be compelled by a greater force of desire that comes from the inside, and this desire is not a feeling. It's the thing that gets you out of bed to pray and study God's Word when you *feel* like you would rather hit the snooze button for the fourth time. It's the strength to keep your mouth shut when you *feel* like you want to criticize your spouse or your children. It sees ahead to where you are going and gives you the motivation to make right choices in order to get there.

2. Discipline. I know *discipline* is an intimidating word, but I need to be honest. It's going to take discipline. It's going to take a ruthless consistency to keep ourselves on the path of renewal. Many people think they are disciplined, but really they are just keeping themselves from who they truly are until they feel justified enough to take a day off and do what they really want to do. For instance, these are the dieters who eat sensibly for six days patiently waiting for the seventh day—"free day"! They really aren't changing any habits because on that seventh day, they go hog wild and ruin everything they've accomplished for the six days prior. Discipline is making the changes. Period. No days off, no free days.

This is the kind of discipline it takes to be a different person and to renew the spirit of our minds. Obviously, there will be days when we slip and fall back into negative mind-sets and habits of thinking, but we don't plan for them. We don't set aside a day a week to allow ourselves to be depressed, angry, and weak. When we fail, we simply give ourselves grace, encourage ourselves in the Lord, and get right back up again.

3. Decisions. We need to decide to think thoughts that line up with God's Word. We don't have to sit around and be a victim to every negative thought or worldly whim that floats across our minds. We can choose to think whatever it is we want. When we find ourselves meditating on worry or fear we can stop and decide to think on God's promises and His life-giving Word. We can set our minds on joy, on faith, on abundance, and on peace.

4. Determination. Don't waver! Because you have been living one way for ten, twenty, or fifty years, it's going to take serious determination to renew the spirit of your mind. We cannot expect to change in two weeks habits of thought that we have been practicing for decades. It's going to take some time, and it's going to take determination to discover God's perfect will for our lives.

5. Diligence. To renew the spirit of our minds, we can never quit. This renewal is not an event; it's a journey. In Philippians 2:12–13, Paul writes, "Therefore, my beloved, as you have always obeyed, not as in my presence only, but now much more in my absence, work out your own salvation with fear and trembling; for it is God who works in you both to will and to do for His good pleasure." Working out our salvation is an eternal journey. Remember, when we became born again, the salvation of our spirits was instant, but the salvation of our souls is a continual process. Read this passage from the Message Bible: "What I'm getting at, friends, is that you should simply keep on doing what you've done from the beginning. When I was living among you, you lived in responsive obedience. Now that I'm separated from you, keep it up. Better yet, redouble your efforts. Be energetic in your life of salvation, reverent and sensitive before God. That energy is God's energy, an energy deep within you, God himself willing and working at what will give him the most pleasure." Selah.

17 | The Garden of Your Mind

W ho is in control of your mind? As you go throughout your day, who or what is the controlling factor of how you think? If we all would stop and honestly assess the source of our thought patterns and mind-sets, I think we'd be a bit surprised. So often I hear people say, "I can't help it when I get so mad." Or "I just can't stop worrying. If I don't worry about everyone, who will?" If you cannot help it that you just put your fist through the wall, or if you cannot help it that you are depressed most of the time, then who *can* help you? If you are not in control, who is?

The truth is, you *can* help it. You can because Paul writes in Colossians 3:22 that we are to set our minds on the things of God, not on the things of the world. If Paul wrote this in his letter, and the Holy Spirit included it in the Bible, then it must be possible for us to do what the Word says: to set our minds where we want them and to fix our thoughts on God's Word. Remember, the process of renewing our minds involves taking all of our thoughts that do not line up with scriptures and exchanging those thoughts for the truth of God's Word. Every Christian has the ability to decide exactly what and how he or she will think throughout the day. To believe otherwise is to reject the truth of the Bible.

When I first became a Christian in the early 1970s, I didn't think this truth could really apply to my life. My mind was so out of control. Trying to grab any one of the worldly thoughts swimming around in there was about as easy as trying to hold on to water. In fact, once, when I thought I'd gotten fairly good at this renewing the mind deal, my mentor, Julius, challenged me to try and focus my mind on one topic as long as possible—to not think of anything else except that one thing. He told me I probably couldn't do it for longer than a few seconds. Of course, I didn't believe him. I knew I would easily be able to focus on only one thing for much longer than a few seconds. I tried it. He was right.

Julius wanted me to realize how powerful my mind really was and how difficult it was going to be to discipline it. That's when I understood renewing my mind was going to be a lifelong process. But through the years, I have seen my life become transformed as I have learned to set my mind on the ways and thoughts of God. Although renewal is a lifelong process, every Christian can engage and learn to discipline their mind and progress. To say "I can't help it" goes against scripture, and it is untrue. Rather than tell ourselves this lie, we should say, "I'm mad, and I don't want to change." At least then we are being honest. We should say, "Today I'm worried and depressed because I want to be. I like being depressed because it's an excuse to not get things done and it makes people feel sorry for me. I like being sad because, that way, I get lots of attention."

The "I can't help its" come out of our mouths because we don't really want to take responsibility for our negative thoughts and behavior. Many people would rather stay the way they are than exert the effort required to change. Most of us Christians, who desire to see God's perfect will evident in our lives, need to realize this is not going to happen only by shouting "Amen, Pastor!" at a sermon. It won't happen just by warming a pew. God's perfect will can only be experienced by those who choose to be transformed by the renewing of their minds, and this renewal is the key to maturing spiritually.

To the degree we will renew our minds is the same degree we will discover the peace and the promises of God. If we decide to renew our minds by devoting 50 percent of our attention to God's Word and dividing the other 50 percent among CNN, *People* magazine, our secular education, and our depressed and negative relatives, then we are going to be frustrated as we find ourselves living day to day in and out of God's blessings. But if we will engage in this renewal daily, as our lifestyle, then as we grow in the knowledge of God's Word, we will see more and more of His prosperity flowing out of every area of our lives. Let's go for 70 percent, then 80 percent, until we get as close as possible to 100 percent during our lives on Earth!

Every Thought Is a Seed

Possibly one of the most essential truths we can grasp in the process of renewal is this: Every thought is a seed that produces an emotion and then an action. I'm going to repeat this because it is so important: Every thought you have is a seed. That seed produces an emotion and then an action, which in turn produces fruit in our lives. Seed, then emotion, then action, then fruit. The resulting fruit, whether it is good or bad, depends entirely upon the seed. If the seed is good, the fruit will be good; if the seed is bad, the fruit will be bad.

In Chapter 12, we read Romans 8:5–6, which says, "For those who live according to the flesh set their minds on the things of the flesh, but those who live according to the Spirit, the things of the Spirit. For to be carnally minded is death, but to be spiritually minded is life and peace." Not only does this passage reiterate our ability to choose where we will set our minds, it also explains what kind of fruit will be produced.

If we set our minds on the flesh, on worldly things, those thoughts are the seeds that will lead us to feel worldly emotions (jealousy, insecurity, lust, greed, etc.) and to act in worldly ways. The fruit of these responses will be death or separation from God. Again, for us Christians, this is not referring to our position in Heaven once we die; it is talking about our lives here on Earth. If our thoughts are always based in the ways of the world, then we will exclude God from our day-to-day activities—along with His protection, provision, and presence. But, Paul teaches, if we set our minds on the things of the Spirit, then our emotions and our actions will produce life and peace. Simply how we live each day will move us closer to God's perfect will for our lives.

It's all about the seed we are sowing in the garden of our minds. Just by looking at the fruit of our lives, we can clearly see what our thoughts are set upon. We all need to take a look at the garden of our lives every once in a while and determine what kind of fruit we are producing: our marriages, children, friendships, finances, health (physical and mental), career, and our relationship with Jesus. If you like your garden and it is producing God's life and peace in every area, then keep thinking the way you are thinking. However, if you see parts of your garden you don't like, that are not bringing forth the kind of fruit you want, you can plant new seeds—you can change your thoughts! By changing the thoughts, you will change the emotions, then the actions, and ultimately the fruit will be transformed as well.

One simple way to recognize the type of fruit you are producing is by listening to the words coming out of your mouth. Proverbs 23:7 says, "As he thinks in his heart, so is he." And Matthew 12:34, "For out of the abundance of the heart, the mouth speaks." Your words easily reveal your thoughts. If your thoughts are seeds of death, you will say things like:

"I'm so sick and tired of my back hurting all the time!"

"How come you always make such stupid choices?"

"Why haven't you kids done your homework? You're so lazy!"

"I don't know why I ever married you."

But if your thoughts are seeds of life, you will confess:

"Thank God Jesus has healed me from this back pain!"

"That's not like you—you are smart, and you always make good choices."

"You kids are hard workers and great students—so let's get the homework done!"

"God blessed me when He brought you into my life."

Each day, are you sowing godly seed or worldly seed in the areas of your life? If you listen to yourself talk throughout the day, your confession will give you the answer.

The Seed Source

At the beginning of this chapter, I asked the question, who is in control of your mind? Obviously, you are the one in control, but sometimes we give that authority over to other forces or we allow ourselves to be greatly influenced by other things. The thoughts in our minds come from four different places: (1) God and His Word, (2) Satan and evil, (3) the world and what is carnal, and (4) self. If we could stop ourselves at every thought, we'd be able to see which of these four initiated that thought. We could easily identify whether that seed was good or bad and, at that very moment, decide to accept it or to toss it away. However, usually we are unaware of our thoughts, let alone the source of our thoughts, and it isn't until our fist punches into the drywall, or until we find ourselves popping another tranquilizer, that we notice something might be wrong. But if we could get to the source of our thoughts and identify where they are coming from, now we really would find some serious power.

For though we walk in the flesh, we do not war according to the flesh. For the weapons of our warfare are not carnal but mighty in God for pulling down strongholds, casting down arguments and every high thing that exalts itself against the knowledge of God, bringing every thought into captivity to the obedience of Christ. (2 Corinthians 10:3–5)

In this scripture, Paul teaches the war we fight from day to day is not of our flesh. This means the issue is not how we are feeling, or what we did, or even the person or thing that tempted us to act in a certain way. Emotions, actions, or other people are not the sources of our problems. The true war occurs in the mind. Our mind is the battlefield and our thoughts are the weapons. Paul is telling us our success in life, whether we win or lose the daily battles we face, depends upon how we choose to think and what we decide to believe.

The "arguments" Paul refers to are any areas of our mind that are trying to compete against the Word of God, any thought we receive that disagrees with the principles of God. The scientist, the college professor, the news reporter, the Hollywood screen star, and the advertising copywriter are all attempting to give us their thoughts, opinions, attitudes, and ideas. The talk-show host or movie producer may present knowledge that is contrary to the Bible, but we cannot just sit passively and allow these thoughts to influence our minds. We must choose to recognize the fallacy of these ideas and not allow them to become part of our belief system. What we believe will determine if our lives will produce fruits of life and peace or fruits of death.

Some of us think we can agree with the world some of the

232 ■ THE 3 ESSENTIALS

time and then turn around and agree with God at other times. Not so. No matter how nice people might be, no matter how many good works they might achieve, at the end of the day, the influences we allow in our lives are either for Christ or they are against Christ. Beliefs either line up with the Word, or they don't. As Christians, we must get sincere in our walk with God and take a hard look at where we are getting our mind-sets and attitudes. If we don't, and we just stay lukewarm in our relationship with Jesus, then we will allow these beliefs to run our lives and we will never experience God's perfect will for us here on Earth.

If we want to produce great works in our lives and leave a God legacy for the next generation, we can't just play church and be nice people. We cannot go through life agreeing with everyone and everything so that we won't rock the boat. We must decide there are some things in this world that are right, some that are wrong and completely against the knowledge of God, and then act according to what the Bible says. These actions are the fruit of our thoughts, so we must always be asking ourselves, "Where are my thoughts coming from?" We don't need to spend much time trying to figure out which of the four sources I listed above are the ones responsible for every one of our thoughts. Just focus on number one: God. If our thoughts don't agree with God and His Word, then they're not going to produce the kind of fruit you want in your life. Life or death? You decide.

> If we want to produce great works in our lives and leave a God legacy for the next generation, we can't just play church and be nice people.

Who Told You That?

Ever since mankind began, there has been a battle going on in the mind. In Genesis 3, we find the very first recorded warfare:

> *Now the serpent was more cunning than any beast of the field which the Lord God had made. And he said to the woman, "Has God indeed said, 'You shall not eat of every tree of the garden'?" And the woman said to the serpent, "We may eat the fruit of the trees of the garden; but of the fruit of the tree which is in the midst of the garden, God has said, 'You shall not eat it, nor shall you touch it, lest you die.'" Then the serpent said to the woman, "You will not surely die. For God knows that in the day you eat of it your eyes will be opened, and you will be like God, knowing good and evil." (vv. 1–5)*

The serpent comes to Eve with two goals in mind: to bring doubtful questioning and to offer her new thoughts. He asks her, "Has God said?" in order to try to get her to distrust God. Eve begins to debate with the devil (never a good thing), and now her mind is open to the attitudes of the world and new thoughts are beginning to flood into her mind. Once he sees she is starting to waver, he tempts her further telling her that she will be like God if she eats of the fruit of the tree. Now what she should have understood was that she already was like God! Both she and Adam were made in God's likeness and image (Genesis 1:26), and she already possessed all the wisdom she would ever need. But now her perspective was changing and she was getting knowledge from the world and beginning to believe maybe God was holding out on her. Were there things to know about life He had failed to mention?

Deceived into thinking there was wisdom she was missing out on, she disobeyed God and ate of the fruit. Verse 6 reads, "So when the woman saw that the tree was good for food, that it was pleasant to the eyes, and a tree desirable to make one wise, she took of its fruit and ate. She also gave to her husband with her, and he ate." Immediately, their eyes were "opened," just as the serpent promised, but the new thoughts, new perspectives, and new visions beginning to flood their minds were from the world, not from God. They began to see things in a different way. They looked at themselves and noticed their nakedness—not that they hadn't been naked before, but now they saw their physical state through a mind-set of the world. They had thoughts they hadn't had before, feelings they hadn't felt before, knowledge they hadn't known before.

They heard the footsteps of God as He was walking through the garden. With this new knowledge came a new action: They got scared and they hid. Who knows how many times they had heard God walking toward them, had even walked right next to Him? They had never been scared or embarrassed of their nakedness before, but with these new thoughts came new emotions, and they now were hiding (seed thought, then emotion, then action, then fruit). "Then the Lord God called to Adam and said to him, 'Where are you?' So he said, 'I heard Your voice in the garden, and I was afraid because I was naked; and I hid myself'" (vv. 9–10).

Of course God already knew what had happened, and where Adam was, but He wanted Adam to realize all of what had just occurred. When Adam answers Him by telling God he hid because he was naked, God asks Adam one of the most profound questions in the entire Bible: "Who told you that you were naked?" (v. 11). God stopped Adam and asked him to think about what he had just said. *Who told you that you were naked?* Adam and Eve had been naked since the day God gave them breath and they had never been ashamed of their nakedness before. Why all of a sudden were they hiding, afraid to be in His presence? Doubting His acceptance? Distrusting their relationship? Because of the new thoughts and new knowledge they now were receiving from the world.

So many of us have beliefs about ourselves that are completely contrary to what God believes about us or to what the Bible says about us. What if we were to take all of our thoughts of doubt, insecurity, and low self-esteem and then ask ourselves: Who told me that? Who told me I was fat? Who told me I was stupid? Who told me I was lazy? Who told me I would never amount to anything? Who told me that?!

Just like with Adam, I think God looks at us living our lives on so much smaller a scale than what He planned for us, and He wants to stop each of us and ask, "Where are you?" Or "Why aren't you living boldly in the fullness and the abundance I have provided for you?" And when we answer Him (like Adam did) with our excuses—"I can't help the way I am," "I'll never be able to do what I really want," "I can't do that because..."—He answers, "Who told you that?" Any thought, any belief, and any perspective you have about your life, your world, and your *self* that does not line up with what the Bible says is wrong! If God did not tell you "that," then you believe a lie, and you will never experience the amazing destiny God has planned for you. Any area of your life that is below the perfect will of God is simply because you believe a falsehood about that area, believing a thought that did not come from Him or His Word.

The devil is not inventing any new tricks to tempt mankind away from the things of God. He uses the same line he used on Adam and Eve. Today, he still tries to suggest to every one of us thoughts of doubt in God, thoughts of distrust in His promises, thoughts of valid excuses why you can never change or be the person you want to be. And the world, with its carnal mind-sets and victim mentalities, follows right behind Satan with its communication about how you need someone else or something else to fix your problems for you, how you will never measure up to its standards, and how you are a helpless victim who deserves to be taken care of. All of these thoughts are designed to hold you in bondage and to keep you living a small life—and against what Jesus Christ died on the cross to give to you.

It's all lies, and it is up to you to stop and ask yourself where your thoughts and beliefs are coming from. If you do not have a New Testament scripture to back up every thought you have about your life, your ability, your relationship with God, and all the promises He has given to you, then what you believe is not from God. But, if you will choose to engage in the battle going on in your mind, you can change it! Just as the passage from 2 Corinthians 10:3–5 says, we can capture, or grab hold of, any thought or belief we have that does not align itself with the Word of God and "cast it down." We can replace that thought with a life-giving promise of God and start on the road to renewal. If we will renew the spirit of our minds, we can renew our self-esteem, renew our marriages, renew our careers, renew our relationships, renew our finances—renew our lives! Let's go for God's best in our lives. Let's renew our minds, so we can start to experience God's perfect will in every realm of our lives.

18 | The Nonnegotiables

I couldn't remember the car accident, I couldn't remember the ambulance ride, I couldn't remember the doctors, the police, or even escaping out of the hospital. I was far too wasted from a drug- and alcohol-induced stupor. Looking back, it's a miracle I am alive today to tell the story, but I'm so glad I am. This experience was a turning point in my life, as I began to think, *Maybe there's a reason I'm alive ... Maybe there is a God who actually has a plan for my life ...* After thirty-plus years of developing a ministry and cultivating a relationship with God, I believe this is one of the most important biblical truths to which every Christian must renew their mind. Once I grabbed hold of this truth and truly believed it in my heart, my life started a dramatic transformation, and my journey toward God's perfect will for my life began.

As I close out this section of the book on renewal, I want to share with you five nonnegotiable truths to which we must renew our minds if we are to experience a successful life on Earth.

1. God has a plan and a purpose for your life.

If you want to possess all that God has planned for you, you must believe there is a reason you are breathing air, a reason you are taking up space on this planet. You are not an accident, you are not a mistake, and you are not a product of evolution. This is how the world thinks and is how I thought for the first nineteen years of my life. I was taught I was a random mutation of evolution, and as a result, I didn't believe my life had any particular purpose. If there was not a specific reason for my existence, then what difference did it make how I lived? If it felt good to my flesh, then I did it. How could it be wrong when it felt so right? This kind of thinking is how people in this world can live from divorce to divorce, can casually abort the unwanted baby, and can live careless lives full of drugs and alcohol. It's the kind of thinking I had until after about my third car wreck.

I had already totaled my dad's pickup truck and my Mustang, so this time, I was driving my brother's little white Comet. Driving down Interstate 5 in a completely intoxicated state, I blacked out and crossed from the outside lane of traffic, over four lanes, to the inside guard rail. I crashed into the sidewall and began to roll end over end two or three times and then flipped the car sideways eight times. Now, I don't remember any of this, but I know about it because of the accounts on the police record given by eyewitnesses. I was taken by the police to

Lakewood Hospital where I was examined for injuries. The doctors determined I had no broken bones and, somehow, had escaped the wreck with only a few minor bumps and bruises. Free from damage, I was now free to be taken into custody. But when the doctor left the room to inform the officers it was safe to haul me off to jail, I left the hospital! I have no recollection of how I did this, but I walked right out of the hospital and headed somewhere, probably home.

Later, I woke up from my blackout on the sidewalk in front of a restaurant that used to be called the Flame Restaurant. I didn't know how I had ended up there, or how long I had been lying there beside the road, but I did know that my car (or my brother's car) was gone. I called home and said, "Somebody stole the car! They must've hit me over the head and gotten away with Dale's car!" My mom came to pick me up, and when we got home, the phone rang. It was the police.

"Excuse me, ma'am, have you seen your son, Casey?"

"Yes. He's right here."

"Well, tonight he was in a car accident and he has escaped police custody."

I couldn't believe it when my mom told me what they had said. Escaped custody? I didn't even know I was *in* custody! I was so messed up, I didn't know I was in an accident or had been to the hospital. Needless to say, the police came to the house and took me away in the squad car, and I still could not remember anything, not even a day or two leading up to the accident. I was totally wasted and had blacked out the entire event.

Days later, my brother, Dale, and I went to the junkyard to look at the car. It was completely totaled, and I was shocked at what I saw. There was not an inch on the body of that Comet that was not smashed, and I remember thinking, *Dang! I guess I was in an accident, a pretty bad one, too. I can't believe I didn't die—how did I survive such a terrible wreck?* I couldn't stop thinking about it, and a few days later I remember wondering if maybe God was saving me for something. A few weeks later I was sentenced to Washington Drug Rehabilitation Program, met Julius, and got born again. Julius said to me, "Big Red, God has a plan for your life." I believed him, and soon after I started Bible school, I met Wendy and we began our ministry together.

Romans 8:28–29 says, "We know that all things work together for good to those who love God, to those who are the called according to His purpose. For whom He foreknew, He also predestined to be conformed to the image of His Son, that He might be the firstborn among many brethren." There is a plan and a purpose for your life. No matter where you have come from, no matter what you might be experiencing right now, you must believe God has a specific purpose for your life. It doesn't have to be anything grandiose by the standards of the world, but because of your life, someone is going to be affected, someone is going to get healed, someone is going to come to know Christ, and because of you, someone is going to realize that God has a purpose for their life, too. You must renew your mind to this truth if you are going to walk in the confidence of God's promises for your life.

To be predestined does not mean you are controlled by God or that you are a programmed robot. It simply means God laid out a detailed plan for your entire life, and now you have the opportunity to choose it or to reject it. You can decide to know His plan and purpose for you and receive the blessed life He has offered, or you can walk away from it and live your life on your own. Ephesians 3:3–5, 11 says:

> *Blessed be the God and Father of our Lord Jesus Christ, who has blessed us with every spiritual blessing in the heavenly places in Christ, just* as He chose us in Him before the foundation of the world, *that we should be holy and without blame before Him in love, having predestined us to adoption as sons by Jesus Christ to Himself, according to the good pleasure of His will... In Him also we have obtained an inheritance,* being predestined according to the purpose of Him who works all things according to the counsel of His will. *(emphasis added)*

God chose you before the foundation of the world! Before He created our universe, God chose you. He lives in the *now* and is not bound to the same limitations of time that exist on Earth. He sees the past, present, and future together as if it is all now, and in that state he saw you and your heart. He saw your desires and what you would choose, and He chose you. You do not need to step out of your house each day hoping and praying that everything will "just work out"; you can wake up knowing you have a plan and a purpose for your life. God has already worked the details out according to the counsel of His own will. You don't have to be afraid you don't know all the details of your future—because God *does,* and He's got your back!

Ephesians 2:10 says, "For we are God's [own] handiwork (His workmanship), recreated in Christ Jesus, [born anew] that we may do those good works which God predestined (planned beforehand) for us [taking paths which He prepared ahead of time], that we should walk in them [living the good life which He prearranged and made ready for us to live]" (AMP). God has a *good* life prepared just for you. He didn't say it would be an easy life, but He promised it would be a good, rewarding, and exciting life. You might go through difficulties and challenges, but you can walk forward in the confidence that God has already provided a way for you to succeed in every circumstance.

Don't allow the devil to convince you that you were unplanned, unwanted, or that your life is meaningless. Your parents might have told you that, but never for a second did God think that. Those are lies from the enemy designed to stop you from living with purpose and a determination to be great. If you will renew your mind and believe you have a plan and purpose for your life, you will be able to accomplish amazing things which will bring glory to God and will leave a legacy to those around you.

2. What is in you, not what is around you, will decide your future.

Where you go in life and what you accomplish here on Earth depends upon what is inside you: your heart for God and your strength, commitment, passion, and vision. The government is not deciding your future, and neither is the economy, the boss, your spouse, not even God. In addition, accidents, failures, and sickness do not control your destiny or change God's plan for your life. Where you will be next year or in five, ten, or fifty years is completely dependent upon what is inside your heart. We talked about this scripture in the Vision section, but it is worth repeating: Matthew 12:35 says, "A good man out of the good treasure of his heart brings forth good things, and an evil man out of the evil treasure brings forth evil things." What's in your heart?

We often refer to athletes in this way: "He's not very fast or tall, but he's got such a big heart!" Or "By all statistics, this team should not be winning the championship, but they have such a heart to go all the way." So many times we see top teams lose in the final rounds because they don't "show up" to the championship; they seem to play by rote and their edge for competition is dull. When you go to your job each day, do you show up full-hearted? Or do you come halfhearted and lukewarm-hearted?

The scripture says the good man, out of the good treasure of his heart, will accomplish good things. A "good" treasure is one of faith, vision, hope, and a desire to do things God's way. As a result, that good man brings forth good families, good influence, good companies, and good works of integrity and righteousness. He is an example for others to follow and an inspiration for those around him.

An "evil" treasure is a "fleshly" or a "worldly" treasure. This is the heart that is consumed with greed, selfishness, and lust, and this heart brings forth car wrecks, dysfunctional families, addictions, and disasters. This is a life that breeds blame, condemnation, doubt, anger, and bitterness. And in a lesser aspect, a bad heart can bring forth a lazy life or a mediocre life: a lukewarm life that doesn't attempt to produce anything good.

What is the treasure of your heart? *This* is what will determine your future, and if you spend your time looking to the government, the economy, or the relative to bring change or improvement to your life, you are looking in the wrong direction. Whatever you don't like about your life, or any area you are dissatisfied with, you must look inward for the answers, not outward. The circumstances around you may never change, but if you will rise up on the inside with faith, strength, direction, and power, you will be able to change how you deal with those circumstances. Even if they never change, you *can*, and then you will overcome any problem or situation that tries to hold you back.

3. If you will give your best, you will receive God's best.

Wendy and I were just two kids in our early twenties when we started this ministry. We truly were one-talent kids: not incredibly smart and not tremendously gifted. She came from a small-town environment and could not even imagine the extent of what we would be doing today, and I was a newly reformed drug addict on welfare. Not the most promising ingredients for success! But we went to work and gave our hearts and lives to God. We laid it all out on the line; we trusted in Him and spent those first years giving all of our best, all of our finances, and all of our energy. As we kept giving our best, God began to give us His best and continued doing so beyond what we ever could have dreamed.

Luke 6:38 says, "Give, and it will be given to you: good measure, pressed down, shaken together, and running over will be put into your bosom. For with the same measure that you use, it will be measured back to you." How do you give of your time, your talent, your treasury? Do you give freely and generously, or just enough so you won't feel guilty? So many Christians are giving with a measure of a teaspoon but they are expecting a return from God with a measure of a shovel. If you are giving with a measure of a spoon, then it will be measured back to you in the measure of a spoon. But if you want to increase in your life, you are going to need to increase in your giving.

Whether it is time, finances, relationship, mentoring, or volunteering, if you will give your best, God will bring you more than you have ever imagined. And your best may not be the same as someone else's best, but this isn't a comparison game or a competition. It's a matter of the heart. Some people give what seems to be a large amount, but it's nothing compared to their potential, while others give what seems like a little, but it is huge for their potential. It's not about what you cannot do; it's about what you *can* do.

Consider this passage from 2 Corinthians 9:6–8: "But this I say: He who sows sparingly will also reap sparingly, and he who sows bountifully will also reap bountifully. So let each one give as he purposes in his heart, not grudgingly or of necessity; for God loves a cheerful giver. And God is able to make all grace abound toward you, that you, always having all sufficiency in all things, may have an abundance for every good work." There are a lot of *all*s in that passage. Do you believe this? Have you renewed your mind to this truth?

Your ability to give is one of the biggest deal breakers for your success in life. God sees your heart, knows the attitudes you have, and fully understands your motives behind your giving. Let's be people who live to give and who love to give. We have received freely from Jesus, so let's give freely to everyone around us. If you will be a generous giver, abundance will begin to flow in your life as God brings you His very best.

4. You must live a balanced life, with godly priorities.

The world bombards us every day with what it believes are the most important priorities. When we buy into its media and propaganda, our lives begin to get out of whack, and we start putting value on things that are not valuable to God. As a result, we struggle, and aspects of our lives become difficult. Have you ever had a car get out of balance? When you drive, you bump around even on the smoothest of roads. It's the same way with our lives; even though our situations may not have changed in the least bit, if our lives are out of balance, everything is harder and takes more effort.

Jesus said in Matthew 6:33, "But seek first the kingdom of God and His righteousness, and all these things shall be added to you." If Jesus said that was what we should seek first, then there must be something to seek second, third, and so on; there must be priorities. God is first, and everything must fall in line after Him. When you seek God and His ways, He will reveal to you the specific priorities of your life, but in general I think this is a good guideline: (1) faith, (2) family, (3) fitness, (4) finances, (5) fellowship, and (6) fun.

Throughout my many years in ministry, I have seen Christians become terribly unbalanced even in their walk with God. They assume God is first (which He is), but then they forget about the other five aspects of life listed above. We have had people stick their entire salary into the offering containers; some gave everything they had in savings to the church. Do you know what we did? We called them up, talked with them, and sent their money back. Most of the time, they were people who were new to the Lord; they had tremendous hearts to serve Him but did not have a mature understanding of giving. If they gave every penny to the church, how were they going to feed their children throughout the month? We were able to help them understand that God wanted a good life for them, not for them to just give all that they had to the church.

Once a married couple with several kids came up to me and said, "We believe God wants us to be at church every single night." I said, "Well, you sure can do that, but Wendy and I won't be here. We'll be here for all our services, and then some, but we also want to make sure we are having time for our children and for each other." If I spent every moment in church, how could I have a successful marriage or raise healthy children or cultivate good friendships? We need to stay balanced and keep godly priorities if we are going to experience all God has for our lives.

Sometimes people put "Fun" at the top of their list. They spend their time at sporting events, playing with their video games, or reading their suspenseful novels, but they have no time for God or for their families. I've seen entire families who are always about having fun in their many activities but do not have the time to sit down and share a meal together or to have godly conversation about their lives. Some put "Finances" at the top of the list. I heard a famous businessman say in an interview, "If you want success in your business, you will not have time for your family." I yelled at the TV, "That's a lie!" You can have success in every area of your life if you will maintain godly priorities. Unfortunately, this man is a self-fulfilling prophecy as he has had three divorces and has to petition the courts to visit his kids.

Proverb 11:1 tells us that God loves a just balance, and when we renew our minds to Matthew 6:33, we will be able to structure our lives with proper priorities. When you seek God first, and make the time to be faithful to your family, your health, and your church, at the end of the day you will see the tremendous blessings of the Lord in every area of your life.

5. Excellence is the way of the Lord in all you do.

"O Lord, our Lord, How excellent is Your name in all the earth, Who has set Your glory above the heavens!" (Psalm 8:1). God is an excellent God. The psalm says His name is "excellent" throughout all the earth. When it refers to God's "name," it means His character, His nature, everything about Him. Throughout the Bible, the names of God describe who He is and give us insight into another facet of His being. Everything He is and everything He does is excellent, and His desire is for every one of us to reflect this quality through the examples of our lives.

Daniel was the epitome of excellence. He was a Jew in the midst of Babylon: a minority, a refugee, and an orphan. The ungodly men around him were responsible for killing his parents and destroying his nation, but he never gave in to excuses or to a victim's mentality. In Daniel 5:12, we see the men of high rank describing him as a man with "an excellent spirit." He had an excellent prayer life, excellent habits, and was an excellent example for his friends to follow. All the circumstances around him were negative, but because of his excellent spirit, he rose up in the ranks and the kings around him took notice. Whenever the nation was in serious trouble, it was Daniel who was called in to help. He never bowed down, never gave up, and the Bible refers to him as one of God's greatest men.

Do you approach your life like Excellent Daniel, or are you a Sloppy Joe, sloppy in your habits, sloppy in your household, sloppy in your eating, sloppy on your job, and sloppy in your walk with Jesus? God's Spirit lives inside every born-again believer, so to live our lives anything less than excellently violates the very being of who resides in our hearts. Whenever we decide to live in a sloppy way, a mediocre way, or an undirected, haphazard way, we grieve the Holy Spirit as He is trying to lead and guide us through our destiny.

We all desire for God to be excellent in our lives, but we will not receive this until we choose to live excellently for Him. Maybe you cannot be excellent in every area, but you can possess an attitude of diligence and determination. Perhaps you are not excellent at math or sales or in organization, but you are excellent at some things—focus on those. You may be like Daniel and have come from extreme difficulties and negative circumstances, but if you choose to possess an excellent spirit, you will rise up, just like Daniel, above the poverty, the tragedy, and the defeat. Let's live excellently in our character, in our integrity, and in our daily walk with God. Let's be great at the gifts and talents God has given us and, to the best of our ability, go for excellence in all realms of life!

Renewal is the last of "the 3" but most certainly never the least! The Renewal Manual, which follows, is one of the most powerful tools I can offer you. It delves deeper into all three essentials—Faith, Vision, and Renewal—and demonstrates how to turn these spiritual concepts into supernatural realities in your life. If you will give yourself to the thirty-day program, you will discover the power of faith like never before and begin to dream dreams you never thought possible. You will learn to think like God thinks and to experience the exhilaration of being transformed into the image of Jesus Christ.

RENEWAL MANUAL

Renewal

The ability to change and renew is an amazing, miraculous
power residing in every Christian. However, while change is
fun and very rewarding, it certainly is not easy. If it were easy,
then every person would constantly be bettering themselves
and overcoming every bad habit they ever picked up. The fact is
renewal is a daily process that takes desire, discipline, and determination—but *you can do it!* And the blessings you will experience because you choose to engage in the process of change will
far outweigh any kind of difficulty. Unlike most people who are
stuck in the mud of mediocrity, you will move toward God's *perfect* will for your life.

This devotional will help you to deepen your faith, clarify
your vision, and confidently embrace renewal for your life and
your mind. Over a thirty-day process, we will walk together, and

each day, will take one step further into destiny. Renewing your mind and changing your life is a daily walk, made up of many parts, and to help you develop the skills necessary to change, this manual is divided into three ten-day sections. The first section will focus on faith, the second on vision, and the third on renewal. Each section offers meditative questions, topical scriptures, and daily action steps.

While this is structured as a thirty-day program, feel free to use this resource in the way that best suits your needs. You may want to use it as a thirty-week program and to allow God to deeply penetrate your spirit and soul with these biblical principles. Or you may want to spend longer times in one section and shorter times in the others. Either way, if you will simply *use* this manual, and not just skim through it, you will begin to experience incredible results. You'll be infused with stronger faith; you'll uncover newer and broader ways to affect others in your life; and you'll finally find the ability to leave behind those negative habits and circumstances that have been holding you back for far too long!

SECTION ONE
FAITH

After more than thirty years in ministry, I am convinced more than ever that faith is the master key for success in every area of life. It is *the* cornerstone and *the* foundation of the Christian experience, and without faith we are unable to receive anything from God. *By* faith we begin our relationship with God, *with* faith we walk every step of our lives, and *through* faith we can see God's promises in action. Faith gives us God's vision to see the impossible as possible. Faith provides us strength to walk through the greatest storms of life, faith orders our lives and propels us forward in our destinies, and faith can change any area, from the smallest to the biggest, with which we are dissatisfied. Without faith, we will never see the full blessings of God, but with faith, we will experience wonders and miracles the world only wishes it could receive. To win in life, you must have faith.

Day 1: Your Faith

Mark 11:23—"For assuredly, I say to you, whoever says to this mountain, 'Be removed and be cast into the sea,' and does not doubt in his heart, but believes that those things he says will be done, he will have whatever he says."

- Throughout reading this book, have you been able to identify the doubts and fears holding you back?

- Do you consider yourself to be a person of great faith?

- Are you confident God hears *and* answers your prayers?

The first step on the journey to trusting and abiding in faith is to believe *you* are a person of faith. Many Christians hear about faith and read about faith, but if someone were to ask for a show of hands from the ones who believed they actually possessed strong faith, a majority would keep their hands down. The fact is every single Christian can be a person with mountain-moving faith, he or she just needs to begin to operate in it.

Hebrews 11:6 says, "But without faith it is impossible to please Him, for he who comes to God must believe that He is, and that He is a rewarder of those who diligently seek Him." Some people stop reading after the first part of this verse and start wondering if they have the kind of faith that is pleasing to God. But the next part gives the answer! If you believe in God— the God you have never seen with your own eyes—then right then and there, you are a person of faith. Just settle this within you right now: Do you believe God exists? Fantastic! You are a person of faith, and you are very pleasing to God.

Then, and maybe even more exciting, now that you have established you are a person of faith, you can also be fully confident that God hears and answers your prayers. "Now this is the confidence that we have in Him, that if we ask anything according to His will, He hears us. And if we know that He hears us, whatever we ask, we know that we have the petitions that we have asked of Him," says 1 John 5:14–15.

Today, spend time meditating on these scriptures. Confess them over yourself, and take a huge step in your destiny by believing you possess the kind of faith that can change your world.

Day 2: God's Love

1 John 4:16—"And we have known and believed the love that God has for us. God is love and he who abides in love abides in God and God in him."

- Do you believe in God's love for you?

- Are you able to daily receive and operate in God's love?

- Does an inability to forgive others—even yourself—keep you from receiving God's love?

Many Christians have a difficult time embracing the depths of the love God has for them. Either because of guilt or feelings of inadequacy or because they think they never can measure up to the person they think God is expecting them to be, they walk through life believing God is angry or disappointed with them. This could not be any further from the truth!

There are a multitude of scriptures throughout the Bible that express the great love God has for each and every one of us; we only need to believe them by faith. In Psalm 139, David writes how intricately and beautifully God fashioned every person, and in verses 17–18, he says: "How precious also are Your thoughts to me, O God! How great is the sum of them! If I should count them, they would be more in number than the sand; When I awake, I am still with You." David truly understood God's love for him, as even in the midst of great failure, the king chose to receive God's amazing grace and forgiveness.

The apostle Paul was another Christian who had a revelation of God's love. In Ephesians 2:4–5, he writes, "But God, who is rich in mercy, because of His great love with which He loved us, even when we were dead in trespasses, made us alive together with Christ (by grace you have been saved)." And again in Romans 8:31–32, 38–39: "If God is for us, who can be against us? He who did not spare His own Son, but delivered Him up for us all, how shall He not with Him also freely give us all things? For I am persuaded that neither death nor life, nor angels nor principalities nor powers, nor things present nor things to come, nor height nor depth, nor any other created thing, shall be able to separate us from the love of God which is in Christ Jesus our Lord."

Today, spend some time meditating on the incredible love God has just for you; let these words penetrate your heart and increase your faith in your relationship with Him.

Day 3: Healing

Matthew 8:16–17—"When evening had come, they brought to Him many who were demon-possessed. And He cast out the spirits with a word, and healed all who were sick, that it might be fulfilled which was spoken by Isaiah the prophet, saying:

"'He Himself took our infirmities and bore our sicknesses.'"

- What is your first response when you encounter sickness?

- Do you wrestle with haunting fears about getting a life-threatening illness?

- When you pray, if you do not receive healing immediately, does your mind focus on fear and doubt?

In our society today, we cannot seem to get away from a constant awareness of sickness and disease. Whether through television commercials, magazine ads, or billboard signs, we are bombarded every day with advertisements for the newest drug designed to tackle the newest sickness, along with its long list of side effects. In addition, many of our most popular television series are based upon the medical field, and with every episode the viewer gets a chance to come face to face with a vivid picture of many different life-threatening illnesses. Is it any wonder our faith for healing can so often become overshadowed by the input from the world?

If you are dealing with sickness, or even if you fight lingering fears of contracting serious sicknesses, ask yourself which occupies more of your time: faith scriptures about the promise of God's healing or negative input from the world? It's time to turn off the television and open up your Bible! In the Faith Manual, I have given you many scriptures of God's promise of supernatural healing for you to speak over yourself. Grab a concordance and look up every scripture you can find about how Jesus healed *all* those who asked. He will do the same for you! Meditate on God's life-giving power that resides on the inside of you. Romans 8:11 promises: "And if the Spirit of Him Who raised up Jesus from the dead dwells in you, [then] He Who raised up Christ Jesus from the dead will also restore to life your mortal (short-lived, perishable) bodies through His Spirit Who dwells in you" (AMP).

God's plan for your life is to live without the sickness and disease of this world. Sure, sometimes we must walk through a valley of weakness in our bodies, but if we will stand firm in our faith, we can be assured we will make it through that valley and into a place of healing and wholeness.

Day 4: Fear

2 Timothy 1:7—"For God has not given us a spirit of fear, but of power and of love and a sound mind."

- In what areas of your life do you find you worry the most?
- Is it difficult for you to cast your cares on the Lord?
- After you pray in faith, do you still allow yourself to worry and be anxious?

Fear and anxiety have become the norm in our world. People have become so accustomed to living with a general foreboding feeling that when they actually experience a sense of inner peace, they start to freak out—and there they are in worry and anxiety again! As Christians, we have a promise from God that we can live our lives completely free of fear. Yes, that means having a deep sense of peace every moment of every day.

Fear and worry is actually a habit—and it can be overcome. What if you were able to capture every thought of fear you had and turn it into a thought of faith? Like any discipline, this will be hard work, but the reward of joy, a sense of well-being, and the ability to always have sweet sleep would be worth the effort. And just like I wrote in the Faith section, once you have worked out these mental muscles, this exchange from fear to faith will become easier and easier.

Instead of worrying, we learn from 1 Peter 5:7, we should spend our energies "casting the whole of your care [all your anxieties, all your worries, all your concerns, once and for all] on Him, for He cares for you affectionately and cares about you watchfully" (AMP).

Whenever you find you have given yourself to fear and worry, make a choice to cast your care on Jesus. Stop and pray, and as Philippians 4 tells us, offer thanksgiving to God as confidence He has heard your prayer, and then *make the choice* to allow God's peace that passes all understanding to guard your heart and mind from fear, anxiety, and worry.

Day 5: God's Protection

Luke 10:19—"Behold, I give you the authority to trample on serpents and scorpions, and over all the power of the enemy, and nothing shall by any means hurt you."

- As a child of God, do you understand the blessings of safety and protection you are now able to receive?

- Do you speak God's protection over your children? Are you then able to be at peace about their lives? Even when you hand them the keys to the car?

We live in a world that is under a curse; therefore, there may be times we must weather the storms of that curse. However, whether it is actual storms like hurricanes and tornadoes, or lack of storms like intense drought, other natural catastrophes like earthquakes, or accidental tragedies like fires and car wrecks, we can trust in God's protection over our families and loved ones.

There is undeniable evil in the world, and sometimes there will be wars and rumors of wars, terrorism, and crime. But you and I have a choice to make: We can either live nervously, hoping we will never encounter anything of the sort, or we can live courageously, having faith in the promises of God's Word. God never brings the destruction, and He will extend His hand of protection if we will have the faith for it. Psalm 91 is packed with promises of God's protection. Use some of this psalm's verses today to help grow your faith!

> He who dwells in the secret place of the Most High
> Shall abide under the shadow of the Almighty.
> You shall not be afraid of the terror by night,
> Nor of the arrow that flies by day,
> Nor of the pestilence that walks in darkness,
> Nor of the destruction that lays waste at noonday.
> A thousand may fall at your side,
> And ten thousand at your right hand;
> But it shall not come near you.
> No evil shall befall you,
> Nor shall any plague come near your dwelling;
> For He shall give His angels charge over you,
> To keep you in all your ways.
> In their hands they shall bear you up,
> Lest you dash your foot against a stone.

Day 6: Finances

2 Corinthians 9:8—"And God is able to make all grace (every favor and earthly blessing) come to you in abundance, so that you may always and under all circumstances and whatever the need be self-sufficient [possessing enough to require no aid or support and furnished in abundance for every good work and charitable donation]" (AMP).

- Do you believe God wants to financially prosper in your life?

- Is having too much money sinful? How much is too much?

- Can you rest in peace, knowing God will meet all your needs, even when you cannot see the way of provision?

God not only desires every Christian to possess a life of financial abundance, He *needs* us to! It is imperative every one of us grab hold of this revelation with our faith because without money, we will never be able to have the kind of influence needed to spread the gospel to all the regions of the earth. For far too long, we Christians have bought into the lie that financial abundance is ungodly and that it is more spiritual to exist in poverty than wealth. Here are some thoughts to strengthen our faith in this area:

What parents would want their children to struggle under the weight of poverty? None! Most parents live sacrificially just so they can greater bless the children they love. Luke 11 talks about how if a son were to ask his father for a loaf of bread, that father would never in turn hand him a venomous snake; if we as earthly fathers know how to bless our children, how much more does our Heavenly Father want to bless His children? Also in Romans 8:32, it says, "He who did not spare His own Son, but delivered Him up for us all, how shall He not with Him also freely give us all things?"

God not only desires us to prosper, but He wants to bless us so that we can be a blessing in turn. In Deuteronomy 8:18, Moses wrote: "And you shall remember the LORD your God, for it is He who gives you power to get wealth, that He may establish His covenant which He swore to your fathers, as it is this day." If we want to establish His covenant throughout the earth, it's going to take massive media airtime, huge resources for social outreaches, and influence in high places. All of this requires money in the hands of regular Christians like you and me. God is looking to and fro to find Christians. In the financial realm, He can abundantly bless people with the integrity to use that wealth for Kingdom purposes, businesspeople with the discipline to make God-inspired ideas come to pass, and men and women who will not allow greed to cause them to stumble.

Let's be those kinds of people! Let's stretch our faith for finances and be powerful ambassadors for Christ in this world.

Day 7: Self-Doubt

1 John 4:4—"You are of God, little children, and have overcome them, because He who is in you is greater than he who is in the world."

- Do you believe in yourself? Do you believe you have everything it takes to accomplish the dreams in your heart?

- When a challenging situation or a chance to move to a higher level in life presents itself, do you embrace it or stand still in self-doubt?

- Can you list five areas in which you excel? Five areas in which you know you need improvement?

Psalm 139 declares you are fearfully and wonderfully made! God has designed an exciting life specifically for you to enjoy; one that is challenging, fulfilling, and fun. Ephesians 2:10 says, "For we are God's [own] handiwork (His workmanship), recreated in Christ Jesus, [born anew] that we may do those good works which God predestined (planned beforehand) for us [taking paths which He prepared ahead of time], that we should walk in them [living the good life which He prearranged and made ready for us to live]" (AMP). If you have any doubt in your mind about these statements, let's use today to strengthen your faith in this area.

All the dreams and desires you hold in your heart are breathed by God, and He certainly did not place them there to frustrate you. His plan is to make every single one of them come to pass, but He needs you to believe in them, in His power to perform, and in yourself. Sometimes it's risky to step out in faith and go for your dreams; there can be so much unknown, and most times, you'll find yourself well outside your comfort zone! But if you will meditate on the above scripture from Ephesians, you will be able to grow your faith in the amazing promise that God has already planned every step of the way.

It's like when I climbed Mount Rainier, one of the highest mountains in America. The guide had already made the summit many times; he understood the terrain, he knew the correct route, and he also knew what to do if dangerous situations arose. Our team simply trusted in his experience, and although it was one of the greatest physical challenges of my life, the view from the top was extraordinary! As you climb your mountaintop of life, you can put your full confidence in God. He will give you all the strength, endurance, creativity, and wisdom to make all the dreams that *He* placed in your heart come true. You only need to believe.

Day 8: In the Valley

Joel 3:10—"Beat your plowshares into swords and your pruning hooks into spears; let the weak say, 'I am strong.'"

- During difficult circumstances, do you press into God and His Word, or do you try to make it through on your own?

- What has been the most challenging season in your life? How were you able to walk through? What did you learn about God? About yourself?

- Do you have people around you who are mature Christians whom you can count on to help walk you through challenges in life?

I wish I could promise you there will be no valleys for you to endure. The truth is every single person will face challenging situations and have to overcome great difficulties. Sicknesses come, loved ones die, projects fail, and people disappoint. There are no certainties for anything in life, except for this one thing: God is always there to help you through any and every circumstance. When we grow our faith in this promise, we can walk through life with so much more peace and comfort—even in the midst of the valleys.

Probably one of the most famous psalms is Psalm 23, and deservedly so, because it is packed with words of comfort and encouragement, as well as promises of blessings. In any time of trouble, this psalm can breathe life into your soul.

THE LORD is my Shepherd [to feed, guide, and shield me],
I shall not lack.

He makes me lie down in [fresh, tender] green pastures; He
leads me beside the still and restful waters.

He refreshes and restores my life (my self); He leads me in the
paths of righteousness [uprightness and right standing with
Him—not for my earning it, but] for His name's sake.

Yes, though I walk through the [deep, sunless] valley of the
shadow of death, I will fear or dread no evil, for You are with
me; Your rod [to protect] and Your staff [to guide], they
comfort me.

You prepare a table before me in the presence of my enemies.
You anoint my head with oil; my [brimming] cup runs over.

Surely or only goodness, mercy, and unfailing love shall follow
me all the days of my life, and through the length of my days
the house of the Lord [and His presence] shall be my dwelling
place. (AMP)

Day 9: World Events

Hebrews 2:12—"I will declare Your name to my brethren;
In the midst of the assembly I will sing praise to You."

- When you hear about the negative events happening in your region and in your world, are you filled with fear and anxiety or is your heart able to rest in peace?

- Do you pray for world leaders and your city and state officials? Do you have faith your prayers will make a difference?

The stock market plummets. A contagious health scare arises. Terrorism is afoot. There are wars and rumors of wars. And everything is going to Hell in a handbasket.

When the media is bombarding you with every tragedy and threatening outcome—and I know I've said this before, but I'm going to say it again—turn off the television, disconnect from the Internet, and open up your Bible. You will never be able to grow your faith in the supernatural provision and protection of God if you spend more time listening to the voices from the world than the voice of God. No matter what is happening around you, there is only one truth that will never change: God's Word.

Psalm 34 is an excellent psalm to meditate upon during times of stress and crisis, and in verse 19, it promises, "Many are the afflictions of the righteous, but the Lord will deliver them out of them all." Notice it doesn't say "None are the afflictions of the righteous," because obviously, this would be false. But one thing we can hang our hat on is that if we operate in faith, God *will* deliver us out of *every* negative circumstance.

> *The LORD knows the days of the upright, And their inheritance*
> *shall be forever.*
> *They shall not be ashamed in the evil time, And in the days of*
> *famine they shall be satisfied. But the salvation of the*
> *righteous is from the LORD;*
> *He is their strength in the time of trouble.*
> *And the LORD shall help them and deliver them;*
> *He shall deliver them from the wicked,*
> *And save them, Because they trust in Him.*
> *(Psalm 37:18–19, 39–40)*

Day 10: In the Waiting . . .

Galatians 6:7–9—"Do not be deceived, God is not mocked; for whatever a man sows, that he will also reap. For he who sows to his flesh will of the flesh reap corruption, but he who sows to the Spirit will of the Spirit reap everlasting life. And let us not grow weary while doing good, for in due season we shall reap if we do not lose heart."

- How long are you willing to wait to see God's blessings manifested in your life?

- When the promise of God takes longer than expected, are you able to stay filled with faith, or does doubt take over?

- Can you keep trusting in God's timing, or do you finally just decide to take matters into your own hands?

Probably the most difficult challenge of living a life of faith is when the promise for which we believe takes longer than we thought to manifest. I do not know why some people pray for a need and it miraculously takes place, and others pray and wait their entire lifetime. I do not have the answer for why some people get healed and why sometimes another does not. Over the course of three-plus decades of ministry, as well as personally walking out a life of faith, I simply have had to make the decision to have faith in God, to not ask the unanswerable questions, and to simply believe in His Word.

I think it is dangerous for us, as Christians, to bring our level of faith down to our level of experience. If we choose to only believe in God's promises to the extent in which we have seen them tangibly come to pass, well, we have now completely stopped operating by faith. Hebrews 11 defines faith as the substance of the things we hope for, the evidence of the things we cannot see, feel, or touch. Faith *believes* in something *before* it has manifested itself in the natural world. No matter what we experience or what we see happening in the lives of those around us, let's choose to have faith in God's Word. If Jesus said it, then let's believe it. If it's in the New Testament, then let's have the faith for it. Period.

"Now, faith is the assurance (the confirmation, the title deed) of the things [we] hope for, being the proof of things [we] do not see and the conviction of their reality [faith perceiving as real fact what is not revealed to the senses]" (Hebrews 11:1, AMP).

SECTION TWO
VISION

Have you clarified your vision? Have you asked yourself this brutal question: What do I *really* believe my life will become? Remember, the vision you have for your destiny isn't what you *want* for your emotions, your relationships, your health, or your finances. It's what you actually believe in your heart that you will have. This vision could be good, or it could be bad. Either way, it is the determining factor to how much success you will find throughout your walk on this earth. The world is filled with people who want their lives to be different, who want to live at a higher level, but the one thing keeping them from achieving it is the vision they possess.

The incredible thing about being a Christian is we can change our vision! If we don't like what we are experiencing in our lives, we can dig into God's Word and renew our minds to the vision God has for us. Let's spend the next ten days refining and refocusing the vision for our life; it is an essential step to possessing a successful life.

Day 11: Vision Versus Fantasy

Habakkuk 2:2-3—"Then the Lord answered me and said: 'Write the vision and make it plain on tablets, that he may run who reads it. For the vision is yet for an appointed time.'"

- Are the visions you have for your life directly related to the God-given gifts you possess?

- Do you have a strategy for how you are going to achieve your visions, or are you only "believing by faith" they will fall into your lap?

- Have you shared your visions with any mature Christians around with the honest attempt to receive feedback or confirmation?

Many people will say they have a vision, when in fact it's simply a fantasy. And especially with all this teaching on faith and how to have mountain-moving faith, it's easy for us Christians to think we are operating in faith, when really we're just trippin'. Let me explain the difference.

In the area of finances, a vision is: "We're struggling to make ends meet, so we believe to move from an income of forty thousand to sixty thousand dollars a year. Here's our plan on how we can do our part to make it happen, and here are the scriptures we are standing on." A fantasy is: "I have no idea how I'm ever going to pay these bills, but bless God, I know someday God is going to make me a millionaire."

In the area of our health, a vision is: "I want to live a long and healthy life, so I'm going to educate myself about how to stay strong in every season of life. I'm going to be disciplined when it comes to eating good foods and to working out my body, and these are promises from God for supernatural health." A fantasy is: "By Jesus' stripes I am healed and made whole, so pass me the bag of Doritos and the two-liter bottle of pop while I sit here and watch TV."

Even if you have what you would call clear and detailed visions for your life, if you are doing nothing to make them happen, then those dreams are simply fantasies. Proverbs tells us that the *steps* of a righteous man are ordered of the Lord—not the butt-prints in the sofa of a righteous man. James tells us that faith without works is dead; in other words, your vision without any tangible effort or strategy on your part is just a pipe dream. Today, take an honest look at your vision for your life, and as we walk through these next several days, allow the Holy Spirit to reveal to you any needed adjustments.

Day 12: Walk with God

Romans 8:14-16—"For as many as are led by the Spirit of God, these are sons of God. For you did not receive the spirit of bondage again to fear, but you received the Spirit of adoption by whom we cry out, 'Abba, Father.' The Spirit Himself bears witness with our spirit that we are children of God."

- How is your relationship with God?

- Does your vision for your life include daily guidance from Him, or is He the one you call on only when you are in trouble?

Our vision of who God is, and how He acts, is crucial to living a successful Christian life. If our vision of God is an old guy with a long white beard and an amazingly large hand poised to thump us on the head the minute we get out of line, then we probably aren't going to pursue much intimacy with Him. And rightly so—who would want to have that kind of a Heavenly Father? Many of us have grown up with a very staunch and religious image of God, rather than the loving, generous, and gracious Father Jesus imitated in the New Testament. Throughout the book of John, Jesus tells us in numerous ways that if we have seen Him (Jesus), then we have seen the Father, and that He never says nor does anything separate from or in opposition to the Father. If your vision of God is anything less than the incredible compassion, love, faithfulness, and sacrifice displayed by

Jesus, then take some time renewing your vision to what is communicated in the Gospels.

God wants to be a part of every aspect of your life, not only involved in the big issues but also in the day-to-day things that crop up. If your vision for your relationship with God is only as a mentor, checking in here and there for His advice and input, then you are missing out on the exciting life that comes from walking step by step *with* God. He did not send His only Son to die for you so that He could have only a casual relationship with you. His desire is to know you deeply and for you to experience Him working in every realm of your life.

Day 13: Church

Acts 4:23—"And being let go, they went to their own companions and reported all that the chief priests and elders had said to them."

- What part does a local church play in the vision for your life?

- Do you believe becoming involved in building and serving a local church is optional or integral for your success in life?

Jesus came to build His church, not religion, not a social club, not man's ways of doing things. He was passionate about the church to the extent that when He witnessed men and women operating within the walls of the temple in an immoral way, He single-handedly cleared everyone out with only a whip! In Matthew 16:17–18, after Peter declares Jesus is the Christ, the Son of God, Jesus reveals to them His master plan: "Blessed are you, Simon Bar-Jonah, for flesh and blood has not revealed this to you, but My Father who is in heaven. And I also say to you that you are Peter, and on this rock [or the revelation that Jesus is the Christ] I will build My church, and the gates of Hades shall not prevail against it."

What an amazing promise! None of the powers of Hell will ever prevail against His church. Notice Jesus did not say Hell would not prevail over God's will for your life, or your family, or your career; He said it would not prevail over His *church*. This means, when we as Christians are actively participating and giving of ourselves inside a local church body, we will be covered under a supernatural umbrella of God's protection—in every realm of life. Jesus has always been about establishing and growing His church. In fact, if your vision for your life does not include being planted in a local church, you really do not have much going in your relationship with God. But alive and active inside His Body, you will flourish like never before.

"The righteous shall flourish like a palm tree; he shall grow like a cedar in Lebanon. Those who are planted in the house of the Lord shall flourish in the courts of our God" (Psalm 92:12–13). If you are not presently rooted in a local church, then find one today. Look for one that has a pastor who preaches the Bible, music that is strong and passionate, and an unwavering pursuit to bring salvation to the lost.

Day 14: Finances

2 Corinthians 9:6—"But this I say: He who sows sparingly will also reap sparingly, and he who sows bountifully will also reap bountifully."

- What do you believe deep in your heart about finances? Is your vision to never get ahead or to barely get by? Or do you envision living in abundance?
- Do you work with a spirit of excellence?
- Do you operate according to biblical financial strategies?

This may be one of the easiest areas to recognize what kind of vision you truly possess. "For as a man thinks in his heart, so is he" (Proverbs 23:7). It might be a hard pill to swallow, but where you are today in your finances is a direct result of your vision. If you don't like that statement, rather than feeling guilty or defensive, take some time to humbly ask God what really is in your heart with regard to finances. If you are not where you want to be, or at least on the road to where you want to be, then ask God to help you renew your mind and your vision to His will for your life.

It is God's will for you to prosper—for *every* Christian to prosper—but you must align your vision to His vision. This includes aligning your actions to His biblical principles. Prosperity is not simply going to rain out of the sky because you are faithful to confess scriptures over your life every day; it takes action, and it takes discipline. Are you faithful to tithing 10 percent of your income? Are you patient to live within your means, or do you allow greed to drive you into massive debt? Do you operate your household inside a budget? Do you know where your money is being spent each month? These are just the basics to having a vision for prosperity.

In addition, when you are working, are you working as unto the Lord with excellence and diligence? Are you an example to your co-workers of integrity and of discipline? If you believe that you will get raises and promotions on your job, then you cannot just pray for them; you need to be the best person for them. If you are a business owner, you cannot just pray for the new deals and the best prices; you must work hard to go after what you want. God cannot bless inactivity! However, if we will go for God's best with enthusiasm and excellence, He can flow with you and give you supernatural favor in your every endeavor.

Day 15: Health

1 Peter 2:24—"... who Himself bore our sins in His own body on the tree, that we having died to sins, might live for righteousness— by whose stripes you were healed."

- Do you expect to get the seasonal colds, allergies, and the flu?
- Do you live your life in such a way that promotes health or that promotes sickness?
- What is your vision for old age—to be vibrant and active until you take your last breath or to be old and decrepit?

What is your vision for when you are ninety? If you are really honest, some of you would say, "Well, I'm not sure I'm going to be alive when I'm ninety." Well, if that's what you believe, that's what you will get. But here's a new thought: Let's make a covenant, and when we are all in our eighties and nineties, let's climb a mountain and take in the panoramic view from the top. Instead of secretly visualizing our latter decades full of medications, walkers, and Social Security, what if we saw adventure, travel, and accomplishing new victories?

Many people live their life like they are dying. I have chosen not to think this way. I'm not going to live dying—I'm going to die living! My life is going to be so full of new projects and new challenges; death is going to be a huge interruption to my plans. And this mind-set actually guides and guards my actions. When

I was in my twenties, I could eat whatever I wanted and exist on little to no sleep. But now that I am in my fifties, if I'm going to die living, then I will need to use discipline to keep this body strong. I've educated myself about health: I eat right, I exercise, and I put time aside to allow my body to rest and restore itself. I speak God's Word over my body, and I walk in faith that I am free from sickness and disease. This vision has become so engrained in me that if my body begins to feel sick, I'm completely surprised.

If you are expecting sickness to be a part of your life, then you have opened the door for that to be your reality. If you are stocking up the cabinet every fall with Theraflu, then get ready to catch the flu. If you find yourself thinking, *I knew I'd get that cold*, or *I was always afraid I'd get that cancer*, then your vision for your health is negative. Start to speak God's Word in this area, and build a new vision for your future in the realm of supernatural health and healing.

Day 16: Marriage

Ephesians 5:33—"Nevertheless let each one of you in particular so love his own wife as himself, and let the wife see that she respects her husband."

- Do you have a vision of a healthy and loving marriage?
- In your heart, have you completely ruled out separation and divorce?
- What steps are you taking daily to ensure a long-lasting, fulfilled marriage?

No person walks up the aisle on their wedding day thinking, *Boy I hope this thing ends up in divorce*. And yet, we know (even in the Christian world) over 50 percent of all marriages end in divorce. How can that be? If no one sets out to get a divorce, if no one truly wants to end up in divorce, why do over half of married couples find themselves talking to their lawyers and signing papers that rip their families apart?

It has everything to do with vision. Most people have left a back door open in their mind. Maybe they didn't leave that door open consciously, but when their marriage faces a trial or difficult situation (which it *always* will), they begin to think about exiting. If in your heart, you are resonating with this right now, it's time to shut every door, every window, and every secret exit you have saved as your "out" when the times get tough. I realize this is a huge task, and I cannot begin to fully express in this short paragraph how to go about achieving it. Start with finding a strong, mature Christian (of the same gender) whom you know has a great marriage. Ask questions, be accountable, and go for God's best in your marriage.

Maybe you don't deal with thoughts of divorce, but you realize you have allowed your marriage to become mediocre and commonplace. Both you and your spouse have let the passion sizzle out of your sex life. It's time to stoke up those embers! Start to date each other (this means *no* kids out with you), talk and share like you did before you were married, and learn to fall in love again. God has given you a gift—I'm referring to your spouse—so enjoy and make that relationship the most intimate it can be.

Day 17: Children

Psalm 127:3—"Behold, children are a heritage from the Lord."

- Is your vision of children that they are a blessing from God?

- Are you dreading the teen years?

- Do you have a vision for strong relationships with your children into their adulthood?

Children *are* a blessing from the Lord! Throughout my thirty-plus years of being a pastor, I have seen many parents regard their children as burdens. They cost money and extensive amounts of time, and they cost even more emotionally. Wendy and I never viewed parenting this way. Sure, there were times we were frustrated, exhausted, or angry (sometimes all at one time), but we never lost sight of the fact these children were tremendous blessings from God. We were honored to be entrusted by God to guide, guard, and govern them, and we chose to thoroughly enjoy every season along the way.

Now that our three children are all adults, we are so glad we stayed true to that vision. Not only have we found the cliché "You blink, and twenty years go by!" to be absolutely true, but also we realized the more we embraced each part of parenthood, the easier it became. And today, we have strong relationships with all three, they all are passionate about God and His people, and better yet, they are all great friends with *one another*!

Love your kids. Engage in their lives. Spend time as a family together. Pray and talk about Jesus together on a regular basis. At least a few times a week, eat a meal together as a family. Support them and encourage them in their gifts. Help them to find mentors and other mature Christian adults they can connect with. As you sow of yourself into these amazing children, you will find your heart more fulfilled than you ever imagined.

Day 18: Emotions

Joshua 1:9—"Have I not commanded you? Be strong and of good courage; do not be afraid, nor be dismayed, for the Lord your God is with you wherever you go."

- When you envision yourself, do you see a person who is in control of his or her emotions or one tossed to and fro by them?

- When given to your emotions, do you justify your behavior with excuses like "Well, this is just how I am" or "I can't help acting like this"?

There is nothing wrong with feeling emotion. God is an emotional being. We can see many examples of Jesus showing and responding to His emotions, and you and I were made in God's likeness and image. Feeling emotions is never an issue—it's what we *do* with those feelings that can become an issue. Ephesians 4:25–27 says, "Therefore, putting away lying, 'Let each one of you speak truth with his neighbor,' for we are members of one another. 'Be angry, and do not sin': do not let the sun go down on your wrath, nor give place to the devil."

These verses give such insight. If we are embarrassed or "caught" or feeling hurt, we are admonished to fight the feeling to lie; rather, we should speak the truth at all times. If we are angry, we should not punch a hole in the wall or become embittered and full of unforgivingness; instead, we are to seek to resolve the situation quickly. Basically, this is saying, whatever the emotion, if it is negative, then make a choice to not react. Choose to stop for a moment and *respond* instead of reacting. Keep God's principles in mind, and decide to act accordingly. This is true for depression, jealousy, covetousness, lust, and the like.

If you will create a vision of yourself as one who thinks through the feelings instead of saying or doing the first thing that comes to mind, you will become that kind of stable, wise person. And there will be much less drama in your life! We *all* could use a little less emotional drama. In addition, you will be set free from the roller-coaster ride of a life led by emotions. Feelings come and go (sometimes many in a matter of moments), but wisdom is a solid rock. Keep your eyes focused on the vision of God's Word, and your heart will never be moved.

Day 19: Success

Joshua 1:8—"This Book of the Law shall not depart from your mouth, but you shall meditate in it day and night, that you may observe to do according to all that is written in it. For then you will make your way prosperous, and then you will have good success."

- Do you truly have a vision to succeed, or do you only wish and hope you are lucky enough to succeed in life?

- Do you see yourself as the head, not the tail? As a winner in life, not a loser?

- If things don't go your way, is your immediate thought, *Well, that's just as I expected things would turn out*?

This is a big one. No matter how much you want to succeed, no matter how much *God* wants you to succeed, if you do not see yourself as a success, then you will never attain it. So many times, we want to blame our lack of success on outward factors: our gender, our race, our background, our education. The truth is there are many examples of extremely successful people who have made significant impacts upon the lives of others and have had far more obstacles to overcome than we have.

The difference between a person who succeeds and a person who does not can be found in their respective visions for success. A person with a clear picture of personal success will have the tenacity to walk through any trial or difficult situation because she believes strongly the only possible outcome will be success. Failure just is not an option for her; even if she finds herself seeming to fail, she will simply use that disappointment as a means to grow bigger on the inside.

You can cultivate this kind of vision for yourself. Consider all the realms of your life, and ask yourself if you truly see yourself succeeding in each area. Pick one of the areas of your life in which your vision is weak, and begin to imagine yourself succeeding in it. Find scriptures promising you God's blessings in that area, and speak them out every day. Frame your future with your words, and very soon, it will become so engrained in who you are, you will begin to believe in yourself like never before.

Day 20: Generosity

Luke 6:38—"Give, and it will be given to you: good measure, pressed down, shaken together, and running over will be put into your bosom. For with the same measure that you use, it will be measured back to you."

- Do you have the vision for your life to affect the people around you? To influence the next generation?

- Do you give of yourself, your time, your finances, and your emotions freely to others?

In Matthew 10:8, Jesus says to us, "Freely you have been given, freely give." This is definitely the way Jesus lived His life; He freely gave *everything* to us even though it cost Him His life. As Christians, we should live our lives the same way.

So often, we can get so caught up with the issues of life—the job, the kids, the sports, the hobbies, the housework, and so on—that we become cocooned in our own realities. We are so busy doing what needs to be done, we barely have time to breathe let alone talk to our neighbor or say a kind word to the person behind the espresso bar. Our lives become all about our own needs, and we lose perspective that there is a world all around us going to Hell.

Jesus admonishes us in Matthew 5:14–15, "You are the light of the world. A city that is set on a hill cannot be hidden. Nor do they light a lamp and put it under a basket, but on a lampstand,

and it gives light to all who are in the house." God needs you and me to be His light in this world, to hold up our light so they can see the goodness of God.

I've mentioned it many times throughout this book that we were made in God's likeness and image. Everything about God is blessing, life, love, and generosity. If we say we are Christians, and we do not live our lives in this same manner of giving, we are actually violating our own self. It is impossible for us to find perfect peace in our hearts and minds because we are at odds with our own belief system. Maybe the dis-ease you sometimes feel inside you is simply God dwelling on the inside of you yearning to be expressed through your life to those around you.

Slow down. Take a moment to assess if you are caught in a trap of useless business. Prioritize your activities in order to ensure all your days are not simply taken up on self. Ask God to show you each day someone whose heart you can make a deposit in. Take the time to smile at the woman handing you your coffee. Look up and connect to those people who are all around you. You will be surprised at the amazing opportunities God will bring your way.

SECTION THREE
RENEWAL

Just because we are saved does not guarantee we will have a successful life on Earth. It simply means we will spend our eternal life in the presence of God. When we became born again, the transformation that happened on the inside was *instant*, as our spirits came alive to God. However, the new birth was simply the first step in our walk with God. Our spirits became new, but now, if we want to live a dynamic, prosperous life on Earth, we must commit our lives to a daily path of renewal. We need to reprogram our minds that have been conformed to the world by secular school, media, and television. It is only by thinking like God thinks that a Christian can find the complete freedom they desire.

"And do not be conformed to this world, but be transformed by the renewing of your mind, that you may prove what is that good and acceptable and perfect will of God" (Romans 12:2).

This scripture has proven to be the most significant and life-changing truth in my life. I've preached this message of renewal for more than thirty years, and even today, I continue to discover deeper revelation of this passage. Let's take the last ten days in this manual and learn to reprogram our minds.

This section of the Renewal Manual is designed a little differently from the last two. Instead of questions each day, I will offer some common beliefs many of us face that are contrary to God's Word. We need to address these areas, acknowledge the thoughts that go against scripture, and begin to engraft the truth into our hearts. Perhaps each one does not exactly apply to your present situation, but most of these are thoughts that hook us at some point in our lives. My desire is for you to understand how the process of renewing your mind works, so you will be able to apply these principles to every area of your life.

Day 21: Change Is Possible

John 8:32–33—"'And you shall know the truth and the truth shall make you free.' They answered Him, 'We are Abraham's descendants, and have never been in bondage to anyone. How can You say, "You will be made free"?'"

- Untruth: I could never change.

- Untruth: I will never be able to overcome this problem.

- Untruth: My situation is unique and way too big to ever change.

- TRUTH: God's Word will always produce results.

This is the very first belief we must renew before we move on to anything else. If you have been reading these chapters on renewal and, for whatever reason, have opted yourself out of this process, you have chosen to believe a lie. There is no problem, no addiction, or no circumstance facing you that is bigger and stronger than the Word of God. His Word works in *every* situation and for *every* person. Here are some scriptures to replace those untruths lurking in your mind:

"Do not be deceived, God is not mocked; for whatever a man sows, that he will also reap" (Galatians 6:7). Basically, Paul is saying, "Don't be tricked by the devil to believe God's ways are false." Then he writes that if a person gives himself to spiritual things, then he will reap the promises of those spiritual blessings, but if a person gives himself to the ways of the world and his own fleshy desires, then he will reap defeat and discouragement. No matter what you are facing, if you apply the Word and God's principles to that thing, you *will* reap if you do not give up.

Isaiah 55:8–11 promises:

> *"For My thoughts are not your thoughts, nor are your ways My ways, says the Lord. For as the heavens are higher than the earth, so are My ways higher than your ways and My thoughts than your thoughts. For as the rain and snow come down from the heavens, and return not there again, but water the earth and make it bring forth and sprout, that it may give seed to the sower and bread to the eater, So shall My word be that goes forth out of My mouth: it shall not return to Me void [without producing any effect, useless], but it shall accomplish that which I please and purpose, and it shall prosper in the thing for which I sent it."*

In other words, there will never be a time when you apply God's Word and it does not come to pass. It may take some time, but His Word *always* produces the promise. You *can* change, and your situation is *not* too big for God's Word to overcome.

Day 22: Complete Healing

Psalm 107:20—"He sent His word and healed them."

- Untruth: Healing is not for everyone.

- Untruth: I believe God can heal me; I just don't know if it's His will.

- TRUTH: It is God's will that all people receive His healing.

This one can really get me fired up, so I'm going to have to rein myself in as I write this; otherwise, I'll end up writing an entire chapter on this. I cannot tell you how many times I come across this wrong belief in the Body of Christ: pastors who teach it is not God's will to heal everyone, or Christians who give up on faith because one time they prayed for someone who was very sick and he ended up dying, or Christians who are facing sickness themselves and do not believe God wants to heal them. These are exactly the kinds of lies the enemy would have us believe; anything that will shorten or decrease the victory in our lives he is passionate to promote!

We must not allow our hearts to buy into beliefs that are not founded in the Word of God. No matter what we see happen in our lives, we can never change what we believe in order to make sense of our circumstances. Throughout the New Testament, we learn that Jesus, as He walked on the earth, was the perfect expression of God. In the Gospel according to John, He says several times and in many different ways, "If you have seen Me, then you have seen the Father." Let's take a look at what Jesus showed us: "And Jesus went about all Galilee, teaching in their synagogues, preaching the gospel of the kingdom, and healing *all* kinds of sickness and *all* kinds of disease among the people. Then His fame went throughout all Syria; and they brought to Him *all* sick people who were afflicted with various diseases and torments, and those who were demon-possessed, epileptics, and paralytics; and He healed them" (Matthew 4:23–24; emphasis added).

Again in Matthew 9:25: "Then Jesus went about *all* the cities and villages, teaching in their synagogues, preaching the gospel of the kingdom, and healing *every* sickness and *every* disease among the people" (emphasis added). Luke 6:19: "And the whole multitude sought to touch Him, for power went out from him and healed them *all*" (emphasis added). And here are several more scriptures telling how Jesus healed everyone who came to Him: Matthew 8:16, 10:1, 12:15; Mark 1:32–34; Luke 4:40, 5:15, 6:17. These are not even the many specific accounts of Jesus healing people throughout His ministry. Clearly, we can see it is God's will to heal any person who comes to receive it.

In addition, just as salvation is for every person, so is healing. Healing was part of the work of the cross! Isaiah 53:4–5 (AMP) says, "Surely He has borne our griefs (sicknesses, weaknesses, and distresses) and carried our sorrows and pains [of punishment], yet we [ignorantly] considered Him stricken, smitten, and afflicted by God [as if with leprosy]. But He was wounded for our transgressions, He was bruised for our guilt and iniquities; the chastisement [needful to obtain] peace and well-being for us was upon Him, and with the stripes [that wounded] Him we are

healed and made whole." And again, in 1 Peter 2:24: "He personally bore our sins in His [own] body on the tree [as on an altar
and offered Himself on it], that we might die (cease to exist) to
sin and live to righteousness. By His wounds you have been
healed."

As I mentioned earlier, I could write an entire chapter on this
subject, and in fact I've taught many series about God's supernatural healing. I'll close with these thoughts: Let's not shrink
our faith in God's Word down to our experience on Earth. Rather,
let's take Him at His Word and enlarge our faith to encompass
His ways! Let's renew our minds to the truth and not stay in our
thoughts of unbelief.

Day 23: True Prosperity

John 10:10—"The thief does not come except to steal, and to kill, and to destroy. I have come that they may have life, and that they may have it more abundantly."

- Untruth: Prosperity is not for everyone.

- Untruth: It is not God's will for everyone to be rich.

- TRUTH: God wants every Christian to be able to give and influence their world.

This is another topic that can get me all stirred up, so once again I will try to stay holy and use fewer words than I might want to. If you want to make excuses so you can stay caught in a barely-enough-to-get-by financial life, then go right ahead. Scour the Bible and find the one or two scriptures you can take out of context in order to support your argument, and struggle through life with never enough money to accomplish the dreams you have in your heart. But if you are anything like me, you are going to pursue God's best in every area of your life—and this includes finances.

The enemy wants to keep us poor because he understands with wealth comes influence and power; if the ungodly are the ones who are rich, they will be the only voices heard in society. But imagine this: What if *every* Christian were prospering financially? The world would come in droves to find out about this amazing and abundant God! *We* would own the airtime on television; *we* would own the media and the sources the world relies upon for its news and information; and *we* would be the producers in Hollywood creating the movies, television shows, and commercials. Think of all that we could accomplish! Imagine the influence for Jesus we would have. We would be an undeniable force to be reckoned with.

This scenario is *exactly* what God envisioned when He said in Deuteronomy 8:18, "But you shall remember the Lord your God, for it is He Who gives you power to get wealth, that He may establish His covenant which He swore to your fathers, as it is this day." God needs you and me to prosper so we will have the level of influence required to spread the gospel throughout all the earth. Money is simply a tool to finance His Kingdom, and every one of us Christians needs to believe it is God's will for us to prosper. Let's get beyond the greed, move past the unbelief, and pursue the finances needed to build His Kingdom!

Day 24: God's Hand

Luke 12:6–7—"Are not five sparrows sold for two copper coins? And not one of them is forgotten before God. But the very hairs of your head are all numbered. Do not fear therefore; you are of more value than many sparrows."

- Untruth: God does not care about the details of my life.

- Untruth: I don't need to talk to Him about the day-to-day issues.

- TRUTH: God wants to be daily involved in every aspect of your life.

With more than six and a half billion people on this planet, I can understand how any one of us can diminish our value to God and think, *With all He's got going all over the world, why would God care about the issue I'm having right now in my life?* I don't know how He does it—how He is able to have His eye focused on every single one of us every moment of the day—but He does. And while I don't believe He cares whether you wear the blue or the red sweater today, I do know He cares about every issue you are experiencing at this moment in your heart and mind.

Many of us had natural parents who, at times (or maybe the majority of the time), were not plugged into our lives and our needs. As a result, we felt abandoned, rejected, and unnoticed. It is so important for every Christian to resist projecting these negative impressions of a father onto our Heavenly Father; God is nothing like this. He desires to be a part of your life; He wants you to engage Him in every dilemma, every life choice, and every moment of internal growth. He dearly loves you and is interested in what you have to say and what you are experiencing right now. Here are some scriptures to renew your mind to this image of God:

The entire Psalm 139 is an amazing psalm to meditate upon and renew your heart to God's participation in every detail of your life. Here are a few of its verses:

You *know my sitting down and my rising up; You understand my thought afar off. You comprehend my path and my lying down, And are acquainted with all my ways. For there is not a word on my tongue, But behold, O LORD, You know it altogether. How precious also are Your thoughts to me, O God! How great is the sum of them! If I should count them, they would be more in number than the sand; When I awake, I am still with You (vv. 2–4, 17–18; emphasis added)*

In Isaiah 49:15–16 (AMP), read God's reply to the suggestion that He might forget His people: "Can a woman forget her nursing child, that she should not have compassion on the son of her womb? Yes, they may forget, yet I will not forget you. Behold, I have indelibly imprinted (tattooed a picture of) you on the palm of each of My hands; [O Zion] your (lives) are continually before Me." Not only does God have the whole world in His hands, He has each of our faces tattooed on the palms of His hands!

Let's meditate upon these truths instead of any other thoughts that would attempt to chip away at our faith in God's love.

Day 25: Total Forgiveness

1 John 1:9—"If you confess your sins, He is faithful and just to forgive us our sins and cleanse us from all unrighteousness."

- Untruth: I have committed the unpardonable sin.

- Untruth: I think I have lost my salvation.

- TRUTH: No, you have not committed the unpardonable sin or lost your salvation. If you had you would not be concerned or think about it.

I'm not sure if these fears come from a lack of knowledge of the Word, past religious teachings that spread a spirit of guilt and condemnation, or a misunderstanding of the grace of God. Perhaps it is a combination of these.

We want to believe there are venial sins, or sins that do not cost us our salvation, and mortal sins, or ones that are unforgivable and send us straight to Hell. But God said we are saved by grace, not by works, lest any man should boast. When I get to Heaven, I cannot say, "Hey everybody! Check me out! Look at everything I did to get myself here." By the same token, there are no sins we can commit that can keep us out of Heaven. It's all based upon our faith in Jesus.

Salvation is a free gift from God, completely independent from our works—and this means good works or bad works. Salvation is given to any person, regardless of their past, their addictions (remember, I was a huge druggie), or their behaviors; it only takes a sincere belief in Jesus Christ. The moment a person becomes born again, they are entirely transformed in their spirit. The human spirit, once dead and unresponsive to God, is suddenly alive to Christ and a relationship with God begins that instant. To ask whether a person who is born again can lose their salvation is like asking if a baby that was just born could now become "unborn."

In John 10:28, Jesus promises, "And I give them eternal life, and they shall never perish; neither shall anyone snatch them out of My hand." This guarantee is again stated in Hebrews 13:5, and the Amplified Bible reads: "For God Himself has said, I will not in any way fail you nor give you up nor leave you without support. [I will] not, [I will] not, [I will] not in any degree leave you helpless nor forsake nor let [you] down (relax My hold on you)! [Assuredly not!]"

I believe the fears of losing one's salvation are based upon this scripture found in Hebrews 6:4–6: "For it is impossible for those who were once enlightened, and have tasted the heavenly gift, and have become partakers of the Holy Spirit, and have tasted the good word of God and the powers of the age to come, if they fall away, to renew them again to repentance, since they crucify again for themselves the Son of God, and put Him to an open shame." This scripture is referring to the person who has experienced an authentic and mature relationship with Jesus, has communed with the Holy Spirit and operated in His gifts, and then has utterly defied Christ, publicly pronouncing that Jesus is *not* the Son of God. This scripture has less to do with the traitor's actions than it does the complete hardening of the heart, and this type of rebellion is very rare.

Most Christians who go back to their worldly friends and lifestyles and who stop going to church simply do so because they have been hurt, don't want to change their old ways, or never planted themselves in their local church. Then, many are too ashamed or too prideful to come back. But this does not mean they have lost their salvation. This would take a sincere confession *against* Jesus as the Christ and *against* the Holy Spirit.

Day 26: Significance

Jeremiah 29:11—"For I know the thoughts I think toward you, says the Lord, thoughts of peace and not of evil, to give you a future and a hope."

- Untruth: I'm just one person, and not wealthy or very influential at that, so my life is not making any difference.

- Untruth: I don't really have any major impact for Christ.

- TRUTH: Your life is extremely significant!

In today's society, we look at the big movie stars, the pro athletes, and the world-renowned talk-show hosts, and we fool ourselves into believing our lives are puny and insignificant. We even take this attitude into the church and think unless we are a pastor of a mega-church or a worldwide evangelist, we aren't making much of a difference for God. This could not be further from the truth! God does not view the world as man views the world, and He does not value the things the world values.

Imagine if David would have believed about himself what everyone else thought about him. In 1 Samuel 16, when the prophet Samuel went to anoint the new king of Israel, he came to David's father's house and asked to see all the sons. David's father totally disregarded David as a viable option for king and didn't even call him in from the fields to meet Samuel. Even the prophet was surprised when God spoke to his heart that none of these strong, burly men before him was to be the future king.

"But the LORD said to Samuel, 'Do not look at his appearance or at his physical stature, because I have refused him. For the LORD does not see as man sees; for man looks at the outward appearance, but the LORD looks at the heart'" (v. 7). God chose David, and he became the most powerful earthly king in history.

You might never know the significance your life has made on the eternity of another, but God does. Your invitation might cause the next Billy Graham to come to church and give his or her life to Christ. Your kindness might be the reason a person chooses to not commit suicide. Your words of wisdom could cause a young person to make a choice that alters their future for the better. Your private, fervent prayer may turn the political leader of your nation to make choices that affect billions of people.

We can never allow ourselves to believe man's applause is the barometer of our success and influence in our lifetimes. Only God's applause matters, and when we give our lives to Him, we can trust He is using us to the greatest capacity.

Day 27: The Process of Overcoming

1 John 5:1, 4—"Whoever believes that Jesus is the Christ is born of God, and everyone who loves Him who begot also loves him who is begotten of Him. For whatever is born of God overcomes the world. And this is the victory that has overcome the world—our faith."

- Untruth: I need to "get it all together" before I can move forward in my destiny.
- Untruth: God cannot use me effectively until I'm completely whole.
- TRUTH: You will never "get it all together."

I'm not trying to discourage you, but you are never going to come to a place in your life where you say, "Wow. Check me out; I've got it all figured out, so now, I can go help some people." Actually, I'm hoping this will encourage you: I've been walking a strong Christian walk for almost thirty-five years, and I am still finding areas of my life I need to renew and flaws or hurts in my soul I need to get healed. If every one of us waited until we were perfect before we started on our pursuit to help other people, nothing for the Kingdom of God would ever be accomplished.

This kind of thinking is just a way to put off the work of the ministry or to make excuses for why we are not doing anything for God. The truth is the moment you became born again, you were a big step ahead of many people around you. And to lead your friends to Christ, you only need to be one step ahead of them! Now, obviously, I'm not advising you mentor a group of men trying to overcome sexual addictions if you just stopped a habit of watching Internet porn yesterday. But you *can* invite someone to church, and you *can* testify to someone about how God is setting you free in your life. Wherever you are in your walk with Christ right now, you have the ability to be a blessing to someone else.

Even the apostle Paul acknowledged he had not "arrived" when he said in Philippians 3:12–14, "Not that I have already attained, or am already perfected; but I press on, that I may lay hold of that for which Christ Jesus has also laid hold of me. Brethren, I do not count myself to have apprehended; but one thing I do, forgetting those things which are behind and reaching forward to those things which are ahead, I press toward the goal for the prize of the upward call of God in Christ Jesus." But he never let his awareness of his downfalls prevent him from going full throttle for Jesus. Let's have this same mind-set, forget our inadequacies, and press forward to help people know Jesus.

Day 28: God's Way

Isaiah 55:7-8—"'Let the wicked forsake his way, and the unrighteous man his thoughts...For My thoughts are not your thoughts, nor are your ways My ways,' says the Lord."

- Untruth: I need to accomplish everything my way, because God's ways might not be good (or fast) enough.

- Untruth: It's okay to pick and choose the scriptures by which I want to fashion my life.

- TRUTH: God's ways are *always* better (and more profitable) than yours.

Who do you think is smarter—you or God? I suppose none of us would be so arrogant to say we think we're smarter than the Creator of the entire universe, but sometimes I wonder if we don't secretly think it at times.

Consider this: Anytime you know what the Bible says about a particular area of your life, but you don't do what it says, you believe your way is more profitable than God's way. At that moment, you must think you have more understanding and wisdom than God Himself. For example, the Bible tells us to treat our spouse and children with love and respect. Whenever you or I don't treat our family members as God instructs us to, we're basically saying that our way is "more right" than God's ways. We probably wouldn't say this out loud (for fear of getting struck by a lightning bolt), but it *is* what we are communicating by our actions. The same is true of how we treat people we don't care for, what we do with our money, our level of concern for those in need, and every other area of life that the Bible addresses.

One of the greatest lessons I've learned over the decades I've been saved is that God is smarter than me! Even if we took all of the wisdom that every human has ever amassed and combined it all together, it wouldn't come close to comparing with the wisdom of God alone. If we only rely on our own understanding and our own capacity to negotiate through our destinies, then we will never be able to accomplish all God's purposes and plans for our lives. We will only experience supernatural strength, power, and prosperity in our lives when we surrender our lives to Him and allow Him to lead and guide us—in *His* way and in His timing. We will do well if we follow His counsel, and this is done by abiding in and operating by the principles in His Word.

Day 29: Intimacy with God

Isaiah 40:31—"But those who wait on the Lord shall renew their strength; they shall mount up with wings like eagles, they shall run and not be weary, they shall walk and not faint."

- Untruth: I can't afford the time to rest in God or to spend the time necessary to refresh my soul.

- Untruth: As soon as I'm done with this season of my life, I'll be able to relax and press into the things of God.

- TRUTH: You cannot *not* afford to spend time with God; He is the only antidote for stress.

In the Old Testament we read about God's people fighting against human foes. These foes were enemies of the work of God who would seek to bring a halt to what God was doing. While the New Testament tells us we're no longer to fight against people, we do still have other enemies that try to stop God's work in each of us. One of the greatest enemies we face today is the giant called stress.

Stress has become such a normal way of life for many of us that we aren't even aware of how damaging it really is. It comes with many names, such as anxiety, worry, fear, and nervousness. It never quits trying to attack and it will invade the life of anyone who allows it to. But there's good news! We can overcome and defeat this enemy by God's Spirit and God's Word. When we spend time in His presence, we magnify Him over all our circumstances, and when we study His Word, we fill our hearts with God's way of doing things.

In John 16:33, Jesus said we would face trials and tribulations but that His peace can be ours even in the midst of great challenge. When you find yourself having stressful thoughts and you feel the effects of anxiety coming on, it's important to think on the promises of peace God gave us in the Bible. Meditate on scriptures such as these: "The Lord will give strength to His people; He will bless His people with peace" (Psalm 29:11). "Peace I leave with you, My peace I give to you; not as the world gives do I give to you. Let not your heart be troubled, neither let it be afraid" (John 14:27). "Let the peace of God rule in your hearts" (Colossians 3:15). Jesus is called the Prince of Peace. Allow His peace to bring change to your life today.

Day 30: The Savior Jesus

John 3:16—"For God so loved the world that He gave His only begotten Son, that whosoever believes in Him should not perish but have everlasting life."

- Untruth: People who are doing amazing works to help people will go to Heaven.

- Untruth: People who live wonderfully moral lives but do not believe Jesus is the Christ will go to Heaven.

- TRUTH: Jesus is the only Way to the Father.

I placed this one last, because at the end of the day, this truth will determine the success of our lives here on Earth. Regardless of how much personal growth and renewal we have experienced for ourselves, if we are not taking as many people as possible with us into Heaven, then it was all in vain. And the false belief that people who don't believe in Jesus will go to Heaven may be the greatest stumbling block for many people to overcome. We don't want to believe that good, honorable, and generous people will spend an eternity in Hell. It's a very popular philosophy today (and has been almost since the beginning of mankind) that we can earn our way to Heaven, and we are seeing even Christian leaders revising their teaching to embrace ideas centered upon the worldly notion that all people are fundamentally good and on a path to Heaven, regardless of who they believe Jesus was.

In the Gospel according to John 14:6, Jesus boldly says, "I am the Way, the Truth, and the Life. No one comes to the Father except through Me." Earlier in this Gospel, Jesus told Nicodemus that God gave His only Son for the world, and any person who would believe in Him would have eternal life, and those who would not would perish. In 1 Corinthians 3:11, Paul writes, "For no other foundation can anyone lay than that which is laid, which is Jesus Christ." These are only a couple of scriptural references of many that reveal Jesus as the only Son of God, Messiah, and Way unto salvation.

It's understandable and compassionate to want every person to spend their eternity in Heaven, especially those individuals who have offered their lives to serve mankind. This is, in fact, the very heartbeat of our Heavenly Father. It is God's desire that "all men become saved and come to the knowledge of truth" (1 Timothy 2:4). However, God is so holy, righteous, magnificent (and any other superlative you want to add here), it is impossible for any human being to do enough good works to elevate himself to the status of God in order to have relationship with Him.

Salvation is a tremendous gift from the Father, and it cannot be earned; it can only be received. Ephesians 2:4–9 says, "But God, who is rich in mercy, because of His great love with which He loved us, even when we were dead in trespasses, made us alive together with Christ (by grace you have been saved), and raised us up together, and made us sit together in the heavenly places in Christ Jesus, that in the ages to come He might show the exceeding riches of His grace in His kindness toward us in Christ Jesus. For by grace you have been saved through faith, and that not of yourselves; it is the gift of God, not of works, lest anyone should boast."

Let's not water down our message or give in to the popular belief that Jesus is not *the* way and *the* truth. The salvation of humanity is dependent upon bold individuals who will proclaim the reality of God's Word, even if it is unpopular. Let's be those kinds of Christians, and let's not rest until we have ushered as many souls into Heaven as possible!

Faith. Vision. Renewal.

There is a life waiting for you that is free from the burdens of stress, worry, and fear. There is a way to live your dreams and to experience deep fulfillment in your marriage, your relationships, your career, and your finances. No matter who you are, where you've come from, or what season of life you might be in right now, one thing is certain: God loves you dearly and wants to bless you in a supernatural way. All you need to do is learn how to operate in His ways and with His thoughts.

"The 3"—Faith, Vision, and Renewal—with these three spiritual forces working together throughout your life, you will have the strength to overcome any obstacle, the endurance to walk through every storm, and the audacity to rise above any circumstance. They have worked in my life for over three decades, and I have seen them transform the lives of countless individuals in my church and around the world. I know beyond a shadow of a doubt that they will work for you, too. You can possess faith to move massive mountains, crystal-clear vision for success in life, and yes, even *you* can change!